LOCOMOTION PAPERS

The
GLYN VALLEY
TRAMWAY

by
David Llewelyn Davies
revised by R.W. Kidner

THE OAKWOOD PRESS

© Oakwood Press 1991

ISBN 0 85361 422 9

First edition 1962; reprinted 1966 and 1974
Second enlarged edition 1991

Typeset by Gem Publishing Company, Brightwell, Wallingford, Oxfordshire.

Printed by Alpha Print (Oxon) Ltd, Witney, Oxfordshire.

Locomotive *Dennis* seen outside the engine shed at Chirk in May 1932. *H.C. Casserley*

Published by
The OAKWOOD PRESS
P.O.Box 122, Headington, Oxford.

Contents

A fine view of *Dennis* on a train seen here approaching Chirk in May 1932; most unusually, the guard's van-cum-booking office is not on the train.   *H.C. Casserley*

A remarkable view looking down inside Hendre Quarry (about 1893) with granite setts being loaded into 2 ton GVT wagons in the foreground. The warehouse on the right was built by the Glynceiriog Wood Blasting Powder Ltd which had previously occupied the site.   *D.R. Price*

The tramway's garter motif; the monogram without the garter was used on the carriages in the early years.   *Photomatic Ltd*

Introduction

The Author counts himself amongst the dwindling band of people who knew the Glyn Valley Tramway when it was still at work. Between the ages of 4 and 11 he lived at Pontfadog, a station on the tramway, and had vague recollections of riding in passenger trains, before these ceased in 1933. The memory of granite trains running until the line closed in 1935 is much more vivid. He attended Pontfadog School, and the playground was only across the road from the tramway; going to and from school involved walking beside the track for 300 yards. This interest in the GVT nurtured in childhood never abated, and explains the motivation for the first edition of this book in 1962 and the much enlarged edition published now.

The Glyn Valley Tramway was one of the few British examples of a transport system that was once common on the Continent, for it was not a tramway in the accepted sense but a narrow gauge railway running beside a road. Its prime task was the carrying of crushed stone for eight miles between quarry and standard gauge railway.

Its route lay in the bed of a pretty Welsh valley and it is important to stress that the line was run in a completely Welsh setting (although the early horse-drawn line did stray briefly south of Pontfaen into Salop). Most of the persons who were its employees, who used its services year round or quarried its mineral traffic, were Welsh and conducted their day to day business in Welsh. As you read, remember that it would be only in the presence of Saesons (Saxons or English) that Saesneg would be spoken. At other times Cymraeg would hold sway, as is still the case.

> *Peidiwch a bod yn hir, yr ydym yn ymadael mewn wyth munud.* (Don't be long, we leave in eight minutes.)
> *Gadael dwy wagan o lechi i mi yn siding Herber.* (Drop off two wagons of slate for me at Herber sidings.)
> *A gaf fi agor y ffenestr?* (May I open the window?)
> *Neithiwr trwsiwyd points yn y Pandy.* (The points at Pandy were repaired last night.)
> *Pob hwyl, a thaith bleserus.* (All the best, a pleasant journey.)

The Welsh place names found in the text can be translated as:

Coed-y-glyn: Wood of (the) glen.	Pandy: Fulling Mill.
Bronygarth: Top of ridge.	Pontfadog: Madoc's bridge.
Dolywern: Meadow of alder trees.	Pontfaen: Stone bridge.
Glynceiriog: Ceiriog glen or valley.	Trehowell: Howell's hamlet.
Hendre: Permanent habitation.	Ceiriog: (meaning uncertain).

A posed photograph of the locomotive Glyn (and crew) captured in the summer sunlight of 1920.   Courtesy *National Railway Museum*

The Long Struggle To Be Born

The Glyn Valley Tramway (GVT) was a mineral railway for all the 62 years of its life, with passenger traffic a useful incidental. It is important to keep this fact clearly in focus when reading its history. The 19th century saw an explosive growth in Britain in the extraction of minerals from the earth, whether iron ore, coal, limestone, roads and building stone, or slate. The area around Chirk, bordering the Shropshire plain, was no exception to the trend, and the local trend-setter was Chirk Castle.

It was slate which initially led to the construction of the tramway. Slate is formed by the crushing and heating of sediment rocks. This causes the rock grains to rearrange themselves in parallel in a compact mass and gives slate its two essential qualities of cleavage and low porosity. This gift of nature has two disadvantages, for slate is usually found in out-of-the-way places, and it is heavy – a cubic foot weighs just over 1½ cwts. In consequence, prior to the 19th century, the market of a slate quarry was limited to the area that could be covered by animals carrying slate panniers, unless water-borne transport was close at hand.

However, in the early 1800s coal was the most important mineral in the Chirk area, though the Castle, as well as owning Black Park Colliery to the north of the town, owned metal mines and limestone quarries, forges and smelting works from Llanymynech in the south to Vron in the north, as well as properties in England. The colliery had been worked from the 17th century; the Castle, which dated from the 14th century, had been in the hands of the Myddleton family since 1595, but in 1796 Charlotte Myddleton, eldest of three sisters, married Mr R. Biddulph, and this became the Chirk Family name for a time before reverting to Myddleton later.

All the Castle minerals were worked by lessees, and the railway at Black Park running to the Ellesmere Canal, at a wharf later also used by the Glyn Valley Tramway, was laid by the lessee in 1811. Royalties were paid to the Castle; it was small-scale by the standards in some areas, but the records show that between 1811 and 1820, 132,723 tons of Black Park coal passed the weighbridge which calculated the Biddulph income. Other minerals could be more profitable; when in 1805 the Castle granted some leases 'to dig, trench, delve, sink and drive, or try to discover lead ore, copper ore, calamine . . .' the royalty for copper ore was fixed at £2 10s. per ton and for lead £1 10s. per ton; this against a mere 3d. per ton for limestone; however the quantities of the last were enormously greater.

Slate had been quarried at Glynceiriog since the 1500s, being done on a seasonal basis as for turf cutting. The market was only local, until in 1799 the Ellesmere Canal reached the outskirts of Chirk, opening up a theoretical market for Ceiriog slates in Shropshire, Cheshire and Liverpool. But in practice it did not make much difference, as the valley did not even have a decent road to cover the six-mile gap between quarry and canal.

The Castle had owned some slate rocks at Glynceiriog. Charlotte Myddleton Biddulph had inherited the quarry in 1820 from the Trustees of the late

Vicar Price of Glynceiriog; the tenant was Edward Jones. However this property was some five miles distant from the main estate and not felt to be of much use. In 1829 Charlotte (now a widow) sold the quarry 'together with three dwelling houses, two roads and eight acres' to John Wynne of Ty Gwynne, Glynceiriog. It was to be 60 years before this, later called the Wynne Quarry, would be connected to the GVT.

There was to be little change in the Ceiriog Valley, though in 1840 a meeting was called, under the Chairmanship of Lord Dungannon, who owned property on the east side of Chirk, 'to consider a new road to follow the course of the River Ceiriog'. John Wynne (Senior) was there as well as the lessee of the Black Park Colliery and others, but nothing ensued. In Chirk itself, the arrival of the Shrewsbury & Chester Railway brought major changes; this had been opened in 1848 and amalgamated with the GWR in 1854. A short branch line was laid from north of Chirk to the Black Park Colliery, now working pits somewhat to the south of the original ones. Later still, a new colliery was opened at Brinkinallt (Chirk Green), first with an internal tramway and later also connected to the GWR.

The Wynne slate quarry at Glyn and two smaller ones to the west of it still had no adequate means of transport to either canal or railway. In the next valley, that of the Dee, there had been similar handicaps but they were overcome in 1852 by the building of a five mile tramway between the quarries and the terminus of the Ellesmere canal, just west of Llangollen. The tramway was built by a 27-year-old engineer named Henry Dennis, who at a later stage became closely linked with the GVT. Brought up at Bodmin, he became an articled surveyor and joined the engineering department of the Cornwall Railway. When aged about 25 years he accepted a job with a mining firm, who presently entrusted him with the building of the tramway just mentioned and in 1857 he went into partnership with his brother-in-law; the two set up as surveyors and mining engineers with an office at Ruabon, a village four miles to the north of Chirk.

One of Dennis' first jobs as a partner was to act as the engineering consultant to a company, Cambrian Slate Co. Ltd., which had been formed in 1857 to exploit Ceiriog slate for the first time on a commercial basis. This company set out to work one of several existing quarries in the small side valley immediately west of Glynceiriog and estimated that an annual output of 4,000 tons of slate would soon be reached; to this end £22,000 was ultimately spent on quarry tramways, incline, water engine, weighing machine and buildings.

Such slate tonnages could only be handled by a valley railway, and the Cambrian Slate Company came to an agreement with the trustees of the Wem and Bronygarth Turnpike Road to create one. This road had been built in 1771 to link the Shropshire town of Wem and the limestone quarry and kilns of Bronygarth, which lay on the southern slopes of the Ceiriog Valley about 1¾ miles west of Chirk. The Trustees wished to extend their turnpike road to Glynceiriog, but had no money, and so an agreement came about that the slate company would provide substantial finances to build the road and, in return, would be given facilities to build a slate tramway beside the proposed and the existing sections of turnpike road as far as Preesgwyn

A superb photograph of *Sir Theodore* on an excursion train at Glynceiriog on 28th August, 1926. Note that almost all the company's carriage stock is present, including the clerestory saloon (10th) and narrow open coach (11th).

H.C. Casserley

station. This GWR station lay immediately south of Chirk on the Chester–Shrewsbury main line and it was at this point that the railway was traversed by the turnpike road, running eastwards to Wem.

The slate company set about producing a Bill for the construction of a private-carrier tramway and said that if anyone opposed the idea the company would withdraw the Bill before it reached Parliament. It was opposed by Col Biddulph, owner of Chirk Castle and its 6,000 acre estate, because he wished the tramway to be a common-carrier, with the result that the Bill was promptly withdrawn. However, the Cambrian Slate Company had to have some form of transport, and so in 1861 the Wem and Bronygarth Turnpike Trustees presented a Bill with the clause 'to grant to the Cambrian Slate Company the right and power to lay down at the Company's expense along the entire length, or portions thereof, of the road, a tramway for the exclusive use of the said Company'.

There was no local opposition to the Bill, but it came to grief in the House of Commons. The Select Committee of the House in reviewing it felt they could not pass the preamble, on the grounds 'they had never before been asked to unite railroads and turnpike roads together and did not consider it their duty to do so now for the first time'. The Bill finally emerged as an Act in truncated form and without mention of a tramway.

Notwithstanding this rebuff, the slate company paid the Trustees half the capital needed (about £5,000) for a turnpike road between Glynceiriog and Chirk and a connecting branch between it and Herber and the existing terminus at Bronygarth Kilns, and in turn was given the right to all the toll revenues for this new section of road. Construction commenced in 1860 and was completed in about 1863, with the road being given a generous width for the possible inclusion of a tramway at a later date. Tollgates were set up at Chirk, Herber and Glynceiriog.

A further possibility was presented in 1865, when a Glyn Valley Railway was promoted by the Cambrian Slate Quarry and backed by the GWR. However, this was not proceeded with, possibly because it became known that a line was being planned by the Cambrian Railways (no connection with the quarry). The town of Oswestry had been served by the GWR from 1848, with a short branch line from Gobowen. Then in 1855 an Act was obtained for a line from Oswestry to Newtown, and other companies soon carried the trains to the Welsh Coast, while an Oswestry, Ellesmere & Whitchurch Railway made a further connection to the east. In 1864 all these small companies came together as The Cambrian Railways, with their centre at Oswestry. There were many plans for further lines, including an Ellesmere and Glyn Valley Railway (E&GVR). It was promoted by Benjamin Piercy, a leading figure in Cambrian affairs, and the Engineer was to be his brother Robert. An Act was obtained in 1866 for the 13 mile line from a junction at Ellesmere station to the village of Glynceiriog. It would have taken a direct route across level country via Wigginton and Chirk Bank to Pontfaen, and then run with the Ceiriog river, for which several deviations were planned to improve the line. The quarries at Glyn were to have connections by narrow-gauge gravity-worked inclines.

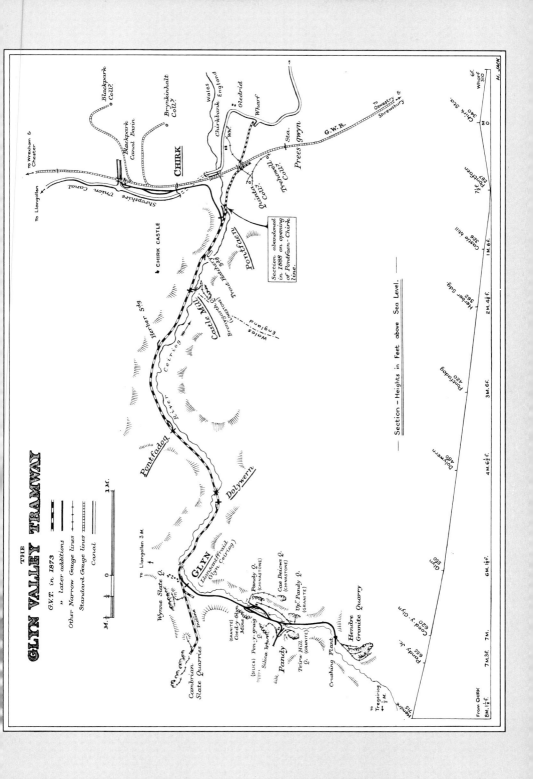

THE
GLYN VALLEY TRAMWAY

G.V.T. in 1873 ▭▭▭▭
" later additions ━━━
Other Narrow Gauge lines +━+━
Standard Gauge lines ▨▨▨▨
Canal ━━━━

M. ½   0   1 M.

H. JACK

Section — Heights in Feet above Sea Level. ━━━━

Unfortunately 1866 turned out to be a traumatic year for the Cambrian Railways. Thomas Savin, who had partly financed most of them and was in fact working them under lease, went bankrupt in February, causing a good deal of confusion and difficulty. This was compounded by the failure of the Gurney Overend Bank, and the railway was not far from financial failure. It was in no mood to go adventuring up the Ceiriog Valley, and nor apparently was anyone else. Thus the slate company was still without hope of adequate transport for its product. No progress was made until two years later.

Henry Dennis came up with a new plan for a narrow gauge line under the same Act from the Cambrian Quarries to Preesgwyn station on the GWR line. The capital would be reduced from £120,000 to £25,000. From a point where the new railway met the GWR, a branch line was to run over the GWR, and 300 yards further on to take over the roadbed of an ancient tramroad which had run from two small coalpits to the Ellesmere Canal at a wharf some way south of Glendrid village. Accordingly the 'Ellesmere and Glyn Valley Act' of 1869 authorised the abandonment of part of the 1866 route and the reduction of capital. It was envisaged that the E&GVR would rent or sell the management of the line to the GWR, the Cambrian Railways, or Shropshire Union Canal.

The Slate Company must have been desperate; a surge in house-building in urban areas was producing a heavy demand for roofing slate, and quarries in other parts of Wales were expanding to meet it. After the 1869 Act the way was open for a railway, but the companies took no action. Fortunately, a new option was to be presented.

Between 1858 and 1861 experimental street tramways were laid in Liverpool, Birkenhead and London but met with such opposition (because of the stepped rail) that they quickly disappeared. These tramways reappeared in Liverpool in 1865, Portsmouth in 1868 and London in 1870, with grooved rails and met with instant success; they gave a quicker and steadier ride than the horse omnibus and the flush-with-the-road track did not impede other traffic.

The benefits of the system were apparent and Parliament in 1870 produced an Act which allowed for the general, but standardised, introduction of street tramways, for up till then each public authority had to obtain an Act of Parliament to enable track to be laid on a public highway. The Tramways Act 1870 specified that a tramway must take the middle of the road with a space of at least 9 ft 6 in. between rail edge and border of the road. It also stipulated that the top of the rail had to be level with the road, that animal power was to be used, and that no vehicle was to project more than 11 inches beyond the rail. This Act stimulated construction and within two years such widely scattered cities as Birmingham, Leeds, Edinburgh, Dublin, Plymouth, Glasgow, Cardiff, Aberdeen and Belfast possessed street tramways.

In the Tramways Act, the Cambrian Slate Company and the promoters of the railway saw that Parliament had conceded the point that public tramways could be built on public roads. The abandoned idea of running a tramway down the turnpike road to Chirk was instantly revived and with commendable haste a further Bill was introduced, which became the Glyn

Valley Tramway Act on 10th August, 1870. Though this Act specifically excluded the application of the Tramways Act, several sections of the latter Act were copied wholesale, including the use of animal traction only and the requirement that rail top and road be flush. Attached to the Act was a memorandum of agreement made between the Trustees of the Wem and Bronygarth Road and the GVT Company which was to loom large at a later date. In obtaining the right to lay a tramway beside the turnpike road the GVT Company agreed to pay the Trustees an annual minimum rent of £150, payable half yearly, which was to take precedence over all other charges made against the tramway company.

The Act allowed for a siding to the Herber lime-kilns, and to those at Brony-Garth (Castle Mill). An extension was also allowed to Nantyr slate quarry. No quarry is marked on the maps, near to Plas Nantyr, and this must refer to a quarry at a by-road junction 1½ miles west of the Cambrian Quarries, which does not appear on the 1880 O.S., but is shown on the 1900 one as disused. It therefore had a short life; it was owned by the Castle. The Nantyr extension was re-authorised in Acts of 1878 and 1885 but was never built. It may be that potential timber traffic from the estate as well as slate was behind this project.

The 1870 Act route of the tramway was a compromise between the routes of the 1861 Wem and Bronygarth Road Act and the 1869 Ellesmere and Glyn Valley Railway Act, and like many compromises contained a serious defect. Instead of taking the tramway on a gentle gradient from the valley bottom to the southern shoulder of the valley about Preesgwyn, it followed the turnpike road from Glynceiriog to Pontfaen, crossed the River Ceiriog on a private wooden bridge, and then climbed 100 ft in 800 yards which gives an average gradient of 1 in 24. This defect ensured that the GVT made little or no profit whilst it was routed in this fashion.

The capital of £25,000, authorised by the previous Act, was unaltered and three years were allowed for the completion of the line. An estimate for civil engineering work and track totalled £14,491 with the latter item costed at £560 per mile of the 'main' line and £480 per mile on spurs. One of the most costly single items was the ½ mile-long gravity incline above Glynceiriog. Whereas the tramway for most of its length accommodated itself to the land contour, here it was forced to run in a straight line at a gradient of about 1 in 8, which called for considerable earthworks when judged by the remainder of the tramway's mileage. It also meant a double line of track, winding drum and haulage cable, totalling an estimated £2,237.

The Act also authorised the charging of certain tolls based, not upon those usually applied to street tramways, but upon those granted to railways, as it was argued the bulk of the traffic would be minerals and not passengers. The maximum permissible charges per mile per ton were:

Coal, limestone, slate, stone, road mending materials, timber	3d.
Coke, bricks, tiles, manure, sheet/bar/rod iron, heavy castings	4d.
Flour, grain, sugar, earthenware, light castings	5d.
Fish, manufactured goods, wool and other wares	6d.

Passengers were not to be charged more than 2d. per mile, and the rental of a horse and car on the tramway could not exceed 1s. 3d. a mile.

The securing of Parliamentary permission in the form of the 1870 Act did not of itself create a company or build a line, as the Acts of 1866 and 1869 had already shown. Although the authorised capital was £25,000 and estimated building costs only £15,000, great difficulty was encountered in raising the necessary money. The Cambrian Slate Co. had burnt its fingers with the subsidising of the turnpike road and had no wish further to involve itself in the promotion of a public tramway. Local landowners, though enthusiastic about the prospects, failed to back their convictions with hard cash. In the end the promoters, still those of the standard gauge 1866 Act, in desperation pared the cost estimates back to £10,000 and made overtures to the owners of the Ellesmere Canal, the Shropshire Union Railway and Canal Company (alias the London and North Western Railway). This latter Company had no railways in the area but used its canal efficiently and effectively to worry the soft underbelly of two of its competitors, the Great Western Railway and the Cambrian Railways. At this time about 15,000 tons of blast furnace fluxing stone and 23,000 tons of coal were moved annually from the Llangollen, Ruabon and Chirk areas by narrow boat to other parts of Shropshire and Montgomeryshire. As the Shropshire Union Railway and Canal Company (SUR&CC) was already carrying slates for the Llangollen quarries, it agreed in mid-1871 to provide half the necessary capital – £5,000 – on the understanding that it would have control over the proper execution of construction work and would be given the sole rights to work the line. These conditions were accepted and on 27th March, 1872, the first meeting of the shareholders of the Glyn Valley Tramway Company took place. At this meeting Directors were elected who included three local landowners – Lord Trevor, Col Biddulph, Richard Perkins – and one canal nominee, George Jebb, the Chief Engineer of the canal. The company's Secretary was John Jones, a solicitor of the firm Longueville & Co., whose offices were situated at Upper Brook Street, Oswestry. This address became the registered office of the company.

Seven tramways were included in the 1870 Act; No. 1 appears to have been left in from the earlier Act, since it was required to cross the Shropshire Union Canal 'by a substantial bridge' and must have been the Ellesmere connection, No. 4, the 20 chain connection to the GWR, was ordered to be opened before No. 1. The gradients of the proposed incline to the Cambrian Quarry are quoted as 1 in: 9, 8, 5, 12, 13, 88. This incline was not in fact ready for the opening; permission to make the line double had been given by the GVT in September 1872.

In May 1872 Henry Dennis, who had surveyed the line and prepared the parliamentary plans, was appointed Engineer, and Elias Griffith, agent to Col Biddulph of Chirk Castle Estates, who had agreed to build the line for £9,442, was appointed Contractor.

The gauge selected was 2 ft 4¼ in. which was, and is, unique among all narrow gauge lines in Britain. It was chosen for no better reason than that is was exactly half the width of the British standard gauge. The track was laid

A pre-1886 view of the terminus of the GVT at Glynceiriog in its horse-drawn days. The scene altered little in the succeeding fifty years for the track layout was subsequently used as a goods and timber yard and shunting continued to be by horse and gravity (see comparison photo on page 18).   *W.J. Milner Collection*

Canal terminus at Gledrid, as it is today, abutting the Llangollen branch of the Shropshire Union Canal. Used between 1873 and 1888 with a track layout approximating to that superimposed. The line of trees in the background marks boat basin, and track in right foreground led to a stone edged wharf at the canal side. The maintenance boat *Lord Nelson* was built 100 years ago of wrought iron and could conceivably have called at the GVT wharf.   *E.A. Wilson*

with flat bottomed rail weighing 21 lb. per yard and spiked direct to sleepers set about three feet apart.

Construction started in June 1872, on the lower section between the canal and Pontfaen, with 50 labourers at work, and was largely completed in nine months. The line was opened to mineral and goods traffic in April 1873 with these observations minuted by the Board of the Shropshire Union Railway and Canal Co., 'It was reported that the GVT was now being worked by the (canal) company at the full parliamentary charges for the present. Mr Jebb reported that in several respects the line was not complete but he understood the contractor would supply the deficiencies.'

At the Annual Meeting on 24th March, 1874, the Chairman reported 'the partial completion of the Main Line of Railway between the Shropshire Union Canal at Glendrid and the Quarries of the Cambrian Slate Company at Llansantffraid. The line to the GWR near Preesgwaen [sic] has also been constructed, although the junction with that Company's line has not definitely been agreed on'. It is not surprising that with the tramway being worked by the canal company, the completion of facilities for passing traffic to the railway had a low priority.

As completed, the railway ran from the foot of the double incline to the Cambrian Quarry to a junction with a short spur leading back into the yard of the New Inn, where sidings and a goods shed were set up (and later a passenger booking office). At a later date (possibly 1884) the Wynne slate quarry, which overlooked the village of Glynceiriog, was joined to the GVT system by a short incline. From Glynceiriog to Pontfaen the track faithfully followed the turnpike road on its southern side with an average down grade of 1 in 110. This meant crossing the stone road bridges at Glynceiriog and Dolywern and occasionally following sharp bends (about the same radius as a medium sized roundabout), but in all places twenty feet was maintained between the inner edge of the track and the far side of the road, as laid down in the authorising Act. At Castle Mill a 300 yard spur was taken across the River Ceiriog over the existing road bridge to the base of an escarpment, on top of which stood the four Bronygarth lime kilns. It is not now known how the kilns and the end of the spur were connected; probably an incline.

At Pontfaen the tramway deserted the turnpike road and between that point and the canal wharf followed almost a straight line route across private land, of which route nearly half existed in the form of a derelict coal waggon way. It charged up the valley side at Pontfaen with a gradient averaging between 1 in 22 and 1 in 30 (with a few yards of 1 in 19) and on gaining the crest of the hill the route lay level for half a mile and then fell away on a gentle gradient to the canal. The terminus at the canal consisted of a stone-edged wharf and basin set at 45 degrees to the canal, which was just long and large enough to accommodate two narrow boats. This installation had served two coal pits some years previously but in the meantime had fallen into disuse. To it was added a triangular reversing set of tracks and a few sidings. This was known as Glendrid Wharf.

At the point where the tramway crossed over the GWR, which was in cutting, by an overbridge built by the former Shrewsbury & Chester Railway, it met the Quinta Tramway. This was being built by Thomas Barnes, the new owner of the large Quinta Estate, formerly owned by R. Myddleton's son-in-law, Hon. Frederick West. The Quinta Colliery had been taken over by the Tre-howell Colliery to the south of it; the latter had from 1868 had a private branch siding, standard gauge, from Preesgwyn station. The Quinta Colliery had arranged with the Shropshire Union Canal to build a loading point at Chirk Bank, and a narrow gauge railway was either built or building to that point, as well as a line joining the two collieries. However, at Chirk Bank the canal was in cutting, and a long chute at the wharf (built in 1871) was required to drop the coal into the narrow boats. It seems that this process broke up the coal, which was not of very good quality anyway, and when the GVT was planning its line, Barnes decided to abandon the Chirk Bank line and obtain a wayleave for his wagons over the GVT to Glendrid Wharf.

The two tramways crossed actually on the bridge, and presumably there was a physical junction, though none is shown on the 1874 Ordnance Survey. A branch of the GVT then crossed over the Quinta Tramway again and ran down parallel to the GWR to the Tre-howell exchange sidings. The GVT had to cross Quinta land to approach the GWR, and it seems the owner was somewhat obstructive at first, but later agreed to the use of his private siding if the GVT paid a transhipment charge of 3d. per ton. This figure was also the charge the GVT was levying on Quinta wagons going to Glendrid Wharf.

There are some outstanding questions on the co-operation between the two tramways; it seems unlikely that the Quinta proprietors would have chosen the same odd gauge as the GVT did, and it may be that the gauge was altered after the co-operation was decided.

In March 1874 the tramway was formally inspected by the Directors of the canal company, headed by Lord Powis. So at last, 16 years after the original proposal by a slate company to build a private tramway, with a gestation period as a standard gauge railway and a narrow gauge light railway, a public horse tramway existed which was being managed by a canal concern!

A train standing at Pontfadog, in the days before the open coaches had their ends boarded.
Lens of Sutton

The New Inn at Glynceiriog was the terminus for the horse-drawn passenger service, the booking office being to the left of the tree. The sidings and goods shed behind remained in use in steam days; the name of the Inn was changed to the Glyn Valley Inn in 1900. *Courtesy Heyday Publishing*

Looking out from the New Inn station, with the line to Chirk going down the street on the right (note the wagons) and the line to the quarries passing across the scene, where the boys are standing. *Courtesy Heyday Publishing*

Chapter Two – Dau
From Horse to Steam

For the first fifteen years of its life the GVT was a horse-cum-gravity tramway and few details of its operating practices and rolling stock now exist. The headquarters, if such a grandiose title can be bestowed upon them, were built in Pontfaen and consisted of a four-horse stable, weighing machine and small office, whilst at Glynceiriog another stable and a warehouse with crane were built.

At the time of the opening the traffic was worked by two horses, but within 18 months these had been increased to eight, which caused the Shropshire Union Canal Company to investigate the possibilities of steam traction. An estimate for a locomotive costing £250 was obtained but the matter was not pursued. Apart from any legal barriers, it seems that animal power, costing the Canal Company 17s. 6d. per week per horse for keep, was more economical.

As to rolling stock, the minutes of the Shropshire Union Canal Executive Committee record in August 1873, 'authorised to obtain a sufficient number of waggons, not exceeding 100, to work the GVT' and in April 1874, 'Mr. Jebb had ordered a suitable open car from Messrs Ashburys.' This second minute relates to a request by the villagers of Glynceiriog for a passenger service which was introduced at the date of the minute. An advertisement in the local weekly newspaper, the *Oswestry Advertiser*, suggests that it was primarily intended for the benefit of visitors and tourists.

> On and after the 1st April, 1874 passenger cars will run daily (Sunday excepted) between Chirk and Llansantffraid Glynceiriog calling at intermediate stations. The tramway runs through the pretty Vale of Ceiriog which is celebrated for the beauty of its scenery and is much resorted to by anglers and tourists. The trains will run to and from Chirk in connection with GWR trains. Particulars as to fares etc. can be had on application to the local manager, Mr Charles Griffiths, Tramway Office, Chirk.

The wording conveniently glossed over the fact that ¾ mile separated Chirk Station (GWR) and Pontfaen Tramway Office (GVT). The reference to 'intermediate stations' was a generous description of setting-down points.

The 'Messrs Ashburys' in the minute was a reference to the Ashbury Railway Carriage and Iron Company Ltd, Openshaw, Manchester, which at this time was producing carriages for British (including the Cambrian) and overseas railways and street tramway cars. It lost its identity in 1902 and became part of the Metropolitan-Cammell Carriage and Wagon Co. Ltd, Birmingham. A photograph taken prior to 1886 shows the track layout at Glynceiriog with a canopied car and three wagons, and an 1891 photo shows a 'toastrack' in the first steam passenger train. These photographs appear to be the only remaining pieces of evidence of horse-drawn rolling stock. It is likely that about 100 wagons were purchased for the horse tramway, for the rolling stock returns of 1888 show 89 mineral wagons and 21 mineral and/or special purpose wagons. Some of these wagons might have been brought by the contractor who converted the line for steam haulage, but the majority must have been horse tramway stock, for the new wagons had yet to be delivered.

TIMETABLE —HORSE TRACTION

From 1st May, 1878, and until further notice.

UP	DAILY (Sundays excepted)			DOWN	DAILY (Sundays excepted)		
	a.m.	p.m.	p.m.		a.m.	a.m.	p.m.
Pontfaen (Chirk)	10.15	1.30	7.15	New Inn (Glyn) ...	8.00	11.00	4.45
Castle Mill ...	10.24	1.40	7.25	Queen's Head Inn	8.10	11.10	4.55
Herber Toll Gate	10.30	1.50	7.35	Pont Fadog ...	8.20	11.20	5.05
Pont Fadog ...	10.40	2.00	7.47	Herber Toll Gate	8.30	11.30	5.15
Queen's Head Inn	10.50	2.10	7.55	Castle Mill ...	8.36	11.36	5.21
New Inn (Glyn) ...	11.00	2.30	8.15	Pontfaen (Chirk)	8.45	11.45	5.30

The Wednesday Market Car will leave New Inn every Wednesday at 11.0 a.m., returning from Pontfaen at 4.10 p.m. On Wednesdays the mid-day Car from Pontfaen will not run, and the Evening Car from New Inn will leave at 5.0 p.m. instead of 4.45 p.m.

Private Cars may be arranged for at Special Rates, on due notice being given.

The Tramway Trains run in connection with Trains on the Great Western Line to and from Liverpool, Chester, Oswestry, Shrewsbury, etc.

By Order,

W. JONES,

Shropshire Union Offices,
    Chester. April, 1878.

General Manager·

GLYN VALLEY TRAMWAY.—Time Table, Oct., 1908.

And until further notice.

UP.	a m			pm	pm		pm	p m
Chirk arr. from Chester	9 44	..		1 22	3 19	..	3 19	6 24
„ „ „ Shrewsbury ...	8 57	..	··	1 19	2 19	..	4 2	6 2
Chirk ... ... dep.	9 50	..	..	1 35	3*25	..	4 15	6A30
Pontfaen ... ... „	C R	—		C R	C*R	..	C R	C R
Castle Mill ... ... „	10 1	..		1 46	3*36	..	4 21	6 39
Pontfadog ... ... „	10 13	..		1 58	3*48	..	4 33	6 49
Dolywern ... ... „	10 21	..		2 6	3*56	..	4 41	6 56
Glynceiriog ... ... arr.	10 30	..		2 15	4* 5	..	4 50	7 6

DOWN.	am	am		pm	pm	pm	pm	pm
Glynceiriog ... ... dep·	8 5	11 20	..	12 25	2✚30	4 5	5† 5	7 20
Dolywern ... ... „	8 14	11 29	..	12 34	2✚39	4 14	5†14	7 29
Pontfadog ... ... „	8 22	11 37	..	12 42	2✚46	4 22	5 21	7 37
Castle Mill ... ... „	8 34	11 49	..	12 54	2✚56	4 31	5 31	7 48
Pontfaen ... ... „	C R	C R	..	C R	C✚R	C R	C R	C R
Chirk ... ... arr.	8 45	12 0	..	1 5	3✚ 5	4 40	5 40	8 2
Chirk dep. for Chester	8 57	12 10	..	1 19	4 2	4 45	6 2	8 34
„ „ „ Shrewsbury ...	8 58	12 11	..	1 22	3 19	5 12	6§26	8 22

G. M. JENKINS,

Secretary and Manager.

Chirk, September, 1908.

C.R.—Will call when required to pick up or set down passengers.

A.—Will wait the arrival of the 2.15 p.m. ex London in the event of there being passengers in that train for the Glyn Valley, provided the train is not more than 15 minutes late. Notice to be given beforehand. ✱—Saturdays only. †—Wednesdays only. ‡—Not on Wednesdays. ·—For Preesgweene, Gobowen and Oswestry only. §—For Preesgweene, Gobowen and Oswestry only.

As for operating practice, goods trains conveying slate and timber would run by gravity on the gentle grade down the valley with a horse and guard riding in a brake box at the rear. On arrival at Pontfaen the train was rolled into a siding and broken into small wagon lots so that the horse could pull them up the 800 yard gradient of 1 in 25. At the top of the incline the rake of wagons was reassembled and taken either to the GWR exchange sidings near Trehowell Colliery and Preesgwyn station or to the canal. In the reverse direction traffic would consist of coal from the Quinta and Trehowell Collieries; tiles, bricks and earthenware pipes made at Trehowell brick works from clay found in coal workings; lime from Bronygarth kilns, and general goods.

Life on a horse-operated tramway cannot be a very exciting business but the Glyn Valley Tramway did manage to introduce one dramatic note early in its life. In the Christmas week of 1874 it threw four passengers into the icy Ceiriog river. The passengers in the accident wrote to the Board of Trade asking for a general enquiry into the running of the tramway and in April 1875 Lt-Col C.S. Hutchinson, an Inspecting Officer of Railways, on the staff of the Board of Trade, carried out an investigation. The line should have been inspected and approved before opening but this was not done until the accident highlighted the omission. That part of the inspection report dealing with the acccident is worth quoting verbatim.

> It seems to be a customary practice both for passenger cars and goods trucks to be allowed to descend by gravity from Glynceiriog to Pontfaen, the speed being regulated by a brakesman. Mr Jaffray, two of his friends and another person hired a special train to descend from the higher to lower terminus on 19th December, 1874. There being no horse or car available they were conveyed in a slate truck, the brakesman and their luggage occupying a second one, and the descent being accomplished by the aid of gravity. During the journey the brakesman is said to have been frequently remonstrated with as to the speed at which he was running but without effect and it is supposed he was the worse for liquor and on the train reaching a bridge over the River Ceiriog, where the tramway near its lower terminus takes two very sharp turns, the trucks left the rails and the whole party were shot into the river, Mr Shakespeare and another being injured. This accident would not have occurred had the Company complied with their Act which provides that all carriages used on the tramway shall be moved by animal power only.

Colonel Hutchinson inspected the tramway in its entirety. He found little fault with the permanent way, but noted in several places that the tramway was raised as much as eighteen inches above the turnpike road, looking like a raised footpath four or five feet wide beside the 20 ft wide road. This contravened the requirement that rails and road surface should be flush, but he accepted the situation because the road was in such a wretched state of repair (and had been at the time of the tramway's construction), that it was almost impassable to wheeled vehicles.

As a result of this affair, the passenger terminus at Pontfaen was moved to the north of the river, on a longish siding running along the Chirk road from the point where the line to the canal swung south, terminating just before the by-road turning to Lodge. Despite this incident, the passenger service,

A fine view of Hendre Quarry in 1962; it was worked between 1875 and 1950. The crushing plant and GVT terminus lay ¼ mile to the left. *Author's Collection*

The year 1898; a typical scene in the Ceiriog Valley looking downstream. The GVT's deviation at Dolywern, with bridge, station and yard, can clearly be seen.
R. Edwards Collection

which ran between Pontfaen and Glynceiriog only, was a sedate affair consisting of one or two horse-drawn cars completing the journey in an hour. The driver announced his arrival at each setting-down point by blowing a horn in true coaching style.

The passenger stopping places were at New Inn (Glyn), the Queens Head Inn (Dolywern), Pontfadog, Herber Toll Gate, Castle Mill and Pontfaen. Fares were reasonable: 1s. all the way, 1s. 9d. return. There do not seem to have been any shelters provided at 'stations'. The time taken was in general 45 minutes down the valley and 1 hour up. However there were some puzzling anomalies in the up direction, in that the up morning car took only six minutes instead of ten between Castle Mill and Herber, and the evening one took 20 minutes instead of 10 between the Queens Head and the New Inn.

Though there was evidence of apparent prosperity on the line with the increase of traffic and the introduction of passenger working, all was not well financially. In the first full year of operation (1874) the receipts were £1,327, and expenses including depreciation and interest were £1,793, giving a net loss of £466. This state of affairs was due to the difficulty of working the stiff climb out of the valley at Pontfaen.

By definition a mineral line must be capable of transporting fair tonnages and here was a gradient that forced every train to be broken into small lots whether the traffic was going up or down. This 800 yards of hill climb sapped the effectiveness and almost all the profits of the tramway for the 15 years of its horse-drawn life.

Each subsequent year the losses continued, but the Shropshire Union Canal held stubbornly to its half investment. The company had spent much money and energy on running the tramway, had built a house and four cottages for its agent and employees at Chirk, had a useful feeder and distributor for its canal traffic, and no doubt felt that though there was no jam today, there would be jam tomorrow. Furthermore there were prospects of new traffic. The building of street tramways in cities made a sudden demand for small blocks of hard stone to pave streets and tram tracks. These blocks or 'setts' were about the size of a large brick and were usually fashioned out of granite.

Granite existed in the upper part of the valley between Glynceiriog and Tregeiriog and in 1875 a company opened a quarry at Hendre to produce granite setts. These were carted by horse for three miles to the tramway at Glynceiriog but again the stiff gradient at Pontfaen made the working of this heavy freight difficult. As the granite traffic increased, so gradually did the slate trade diminish, to the extent that the management committee of the canal company became worried in April 1878 at the excessive stock of Cambrian Co. slates held at its canal-railway interchange depot at Calverley (a dozen miles SE of Chester). The precise cause of this decline is not known. In March 1880 the quarry company asked if it could cease paying rent for its office at Glendrid Wharf.

The Engineer of the GVT Co. saw that the only solution was to convert to steam traction and ease the climb out of the valley at Chirk. Accordingly he surveyed a new route which took the line up the north side of the valley at

GLYN VALLEY STEAM TRAM.

1671) and a particularly beautiful one of Lady Henrietta Williams Wynn (*d.* 1769). *For Wynnstay, see p.* 20.

For the railway between **Ellesmere** and **Wrexham**, *see p.* 78.

Ruabon to Chirk (rail, 4½ *m.*) ; thence by "**Glyn Valley Steam Tram**" to **Glynceiriog**, 6½ *m., from Chirk.*

This pleasant little route affords an agreeable variant to those who are in no great hurry to get to Llangollen. Send your traps on from Ruabon direct, and walk the 3½ miles over the hill from Glynceiriog to Llangollen—too steep for ordinary carriages, but a very interesting stroll.

There are about five trains a day on the tram-road, accomplishing the distance in 40 minutes, and running in connection with G.W. trains from Chester and Shrewsbury. The line is on a "toy gauge" with open and closed carriages. The station at Chirk adjoins that of the G.W. (down side).

Fares :—*Single,* 1*s.* 4*d.* and 8*d.* ; *return,* 2*s.* 6*d.,* 1*s.* 2*d.*

Descending at a steep gradient through Chirk Castle Park the line enters the road at **Pontfaen**, ¾ *m.*, the first stopping-place. Thence it hugs the left-hand fence of the road for the whole distance except for a few yards near the last station. The glen is winding and prettily wooded throughout. At **Castle Mill**, 2 *m.*, we are 10 minutes' walk from Chirk Castle (*p.* 21), open M., W., and F. from May 1st to Sept. 30th. Continuing alongside the Ceiriog we come to (4 *m.*) **Pontfadog**, one of the most picturesque spots on the route. Near it is a fine old oak. Then passing (5½ *m.*) **Dolywern**, at and near which are one or two inns, we come to the terminus at **Glynceiriog** (500 *ft.* ; Chirk is 350).

The *Glyn Valley Hotel* at Glynceiriog (abt. 42*s.* a week) is an excellent house, with good fishing, free as far as Pontfadog, from the industries of the place, which is locally called "Glyn" (address "Glyn, Ruabon") but properly "Llansaintffraid Glynceiriog !" Two miles beyond it are the Glynceiriog and Teirw Hill Stone-quarries.

For the route on to **Llanarmon** *and* **Llanrhaiadr-yn-Mochnant** (*for Pistyll Rhaiadr*) *see p.* 19.

For Llangollen ascend the very steep hill past the church, which has yew trees around it. In a mile you come to cross-roads close to a substantial farm-house. *Bryn-y-Groes*, and the summit-level (1,280 *ft.*) is a little further. Thence, after an almost level stretch you descend steeply to **Llangollen**, and in this direction there is no chance of error. The view across the valley, with Castell Dinas Bran and Eglwyseg Rocks behind the town and Moel-y-Gamelin away to the left, is very charming. The town is entered close to the "Grapes." The principal hotels are on or near the way to the station.

Ruabon Station (*Ref.-rm.* over bridge) is on high ground (370 *ft.*), and from it to Llangollen, a little short of which the level of the Dee valley is reached, there is a descent of almost 100 feet. At first the line passes through the mining and quarrying district of *Acrefair* (*pron.* "Akryvire"). During the descent there is a good view on the left hand across the valley, the railway viaduct of the main Shrewsbury and Chester line and the aqueduct of the Ellesmere canal being conspicuous. The latter, called *Pont-y-Cysylltau*, was constructed by Telford between the years 1795 and 1805 at a cost of nearly £50,000. It is 120 feet above the river, and has 19 arches of a total length of about 350 yards.

Two miles short of Llangollen we reach the side of the Dee. On the right are the limestone bluffs called Eglwyseg Rocks, and then *Dinas Bran*, crowned by its rude castle, rises like a pyramid ; while on the left is the prettily wooded little hill called *Pen-y-Coed.* **Llangollen** is approached by a narrow dell occu-

Details of the Glyn Valley Tramway were given in Baddeley & Ward's *Guide to North Wales, Part 2*; this extract is from the 1909 edition.

Chirk to the GWR station and the canal beyond it. But this route touched the fringe of Chirk Castle park and was opposed by Col Biddulph, who saw it as a spoilation of his land. An earlier proposal to reach Chirk had simply followed the turnpike road, which offered gradients as severe as those being encountered on the existing route on the opposite side of the valley. Backing out of the re-routing matter, the GVT Co. launched another Bill in 1878 asking for powers to work the tramway with steam locomotives. The Bill also asked leave to skirt the village of Dolywern with its severe S-bend and to continue the tramway up the valley beyond Glynceiriog for another 3¼ miles to the village of Tregeiriog. This extension would not follow the road, which now clung to the hillside, but would lie in the valley bottom, for its object was to serve the Hendre granite quarry which lay on its route. Finally, the Bill contained an agreement made between the Wem and Bronygarth Road Trustees and the GVT Co. on 11th March, 1878. This provided that the trustees would be paid £1,000 within six months of the introduction of steam locomotives and once paid the GVT Co. was to be released forever from its obligation to pay an annual rental of £150. As the trustees had not received their rent in recent years and their road was 'in a state of great disrepair', the agreement was not all one-sided.

Parliament was convinced, correctly, that steam traction could not effectively operate the Pontfaen gradient and in the Glyn Valley Tramway Act of 1878 authorised all the proposals except the use of steam traction. It is easy to be wise after the event, but it does seem foolish of the company to have persevered with the idea of steam traction on the old route to the point of submitting a Parliamentary Bill, and reflects little credit on its Engineer, Henry Dennis. Naturally enough the capital required for this extra route mileage was not forthcoming and nothing was done.

The end of the 1870s was a period of strained relations between the shareholders of the GVT Co. and the Shropshire Union Canal as the tramway managers. The shareholders grumbled about the lack of dividends, mis-management, and the arrogance of the large organisation. To substantiate the last point they drew attention to the fact that in 1877 and 1878 the annual general meeting of the GVT Co. was held in the Boardroom of the LNWR at Euston Station, instead of the more workday surroundings of a solicitor's office in Oswestry. They also complained that the canal company was obstructing the flow of interchange traffic between the GVT and the GWR. In turn the Shropshire Union Canal Co. found the situation irritating, for although it had the day-to-day responsibility of running the tramway it did not have complete financial control.

The upshot was the serious consideration by the Shropshire Union Canal in 1879 of converting the line to steam traction and building a new approach route to Chirk. 1879 is an important date in tramway history for it was in this year that Parliament allowed mechanical traction to be used on street tramways. Nothing came of the steam traction idea, and then the GVT Co. proposed that the canal company should sell all its shares to the GVT Co. or vice versa. Tiring of the losses and the acrimony, the Shropshire Union Canal Co. decided to surrender its management of the line, and sell the works and plant it had built at a cost of £4,630 to the GVT Co. for £2,000. The

A canal barge alongside the Glyn Valley Tramway wharf at Black Park about 1906. The view is looking towards the main canal beyond the bridge.   *J. Foster Petrie*

The coalyard at Glynceiriog looking up the valley, c.1930. The station lies immediately behind the camera.   *Author's Collection*

transfer of management took place on 31st August, 1881, after the canal company had lost £7,061 in operating the tramway for eight years. Although no more direct losses would be made, the company fully realised that it would lose much, if not all, of the tramway's traffic to the GWR despite the fact it still owned 50 per cent of the capital of the GVT Co.

The £2,000 paid by the GVT Co. for physical assets had in fact come from the Glyn Ceiriog Granite Co. Ltd, which was the firm working the granite quarry at Hendre. This quarry was producing setts of good quality stone and had an assured market, but it was embarrassed by the lack of railway transport. The company had amongst its Directors, Col Biddulph, Henry Dennis, a local coal proprietor, a gentleman of leisure from Oswestry, a Shrewsbury mineral agent, and a surgeon, all of whom had invested at least £500 in the concern which had an authorised capital of £30,000.

From this time on the finances and fortunes of the Glyn Valley Tramway, Hendre granite quarry, and in particular Henry Dennis, were closely linked. At this period the Glyn Valley Tramway Co. and the Glyn Ceiriog Granite Co. Ltd could be considered one and the same for practical purposes but financial severance came within 10 years. In the first year of GVT Co. managership (1882) 10,000 tons of granite went down the valley as setts and blocks, much of it going to Birmingham, Wolverhampton and Wigan for paving tramlined streets. This amount of traffic converted the previous operating losses to a profit of £15 for the year despite the charge of £2,000 working expenses by the Granite Company.

This was the year in which granite gained ascendancy over slate tonnages, a situation which was never to change. In 1881 the slate quarries had closed and in the following year the Cambrian Slate Company went into liquidation, owing the Shropshire Union Canal £74 in carrying dues and leaving many unsold slates on its wharves.

The Cambrian Quarry was later re-opened and by 1891, having spent money on opening new underground chambers it was producing a reasonable tonnage. The Ordnance maps after this date, marked it as 'New Cambrian Quarry'.

The traffic successes of 1882 were not to be repeated. Other granite quarries were opening up closer to cities and towns in places where there was no need to cart the stone by road and then on an inefficient tramway. The next five years saw little slate, and a sharp decline in granite traffic. This pattern all the more strongly emphasised the need to continue the line to the granite quarry, re-align the Chirk section and change to steam traction if the quarry and the tramway were to be worked for profit.

If there was a decline in down traffic, up traffic remained steady, for it was the easiest way to take coal and goods up the valley. Some waybills dated September 1881 are preserved in the Ceiriog Memorial Institute at Glyn-ceiriog and give an idea of the merchandise carried by the tramway. The bills are printed forms used by boatmen on the Shropshire Union Canal with the words 'Glyn Valley Tramway Co.' superimposed in ink handwriting, and the names of the tram horse drivers appear in the space marked 'master (of a narrow boat)'. On one day both up trams started from Pontfaen, one carrying mineral water for the New Inn at Glynceiriog and 20 cwt. of coal, and the other loaded with bales, a coil of pipe and 1 cwt. parcel. On the following day one tram train started at Pontfaen, carrying 5 tons 6 cwt. of coal destined for Glynceiriog and Pandy, and meal, corn and bran for Llanarmon, whilst a second one started at the canal wharf loaded with 1 ton 4 cwt. of flour for Glynceiriog.

Quinta Colliery and Trehowell Colliery and Brickworks sent some of the products up the valley, but after 1880 this traffic decreased, for in that year Quinta Colliery closed and the coal coming from Trehowell Colliery became more inferior the longer the pit was worked. In 1882 the tramway carried up-valley 814 tons of coal, bricks, and earthen drainage pipes from these works, but these tonnages had fallen to 498 tons by 1884.

David Lomax, the lessee of Trehowell Colliery, Brick & Clay Works from 1868, gave evidence before a House of Commons Committee in 1885 to the effect that 'the Glyn Valley Tramway takes the Quinta traffic at 10.0 am and later I take it by cart' (this refers to traffic to the canal). 'I have carted more to the Canal than sent by Tramway' he said. In a somewhat muddled transcript, he continues 'GWR traffic is transhipped onto my standard gauge branch line and is transhipped out of the tram into GWR trucks. GWR pays me 3d. a ton for transhipment.' This only makes sense if one assumes that the 1st and 3rd 'GWR' should read 'GVT'. It seems from this that the GVT did not have its own exchange facility, and the payment was required for having the GWR truck which was to receive GVT traffic using the Quinta private standard-gauge siding.

A GWR track-plan dated 1884 has survived showing a complex exchange siding between itself and the two tramways north of the Chirk–Preesgwyn road bridge, but there is no evidence in OS maps or on the ground that this was constructed. The Quinta tramway reached its siding south of that road by a tunnel beneath its approach to the bridge and this may have been used for GVT traffic.

Coal of better quality was taken by cart from Black Park Colliery (1 m. north of Chirk) to Pontfaen and there loaded into trucks, as suggested by one of the waybills mentioned above. The toll charged for coal by the tramway company was 6d. per ton per mile, or twice that authorised by Parliament, so that whereas coal cost 8s. 6d. a ton at pithead it had become 11s. 6d. on arrival at Glynceiriog – only six miles away from a coalfield!

The passenger service on the Glyn Valley Tramway, opened in 1874 between Pontfaen and Glyn, continued to operate until 31st March, 1886 when it was abandoned. For most of this period the service consisted of three cars in each direction daily except Sunday, taking one hour on the up journey and three-quarters of an hour on the down run. The first car left Glyn at 8.0 am and the last car returned there at 8.15 pm; these and other times first appeared in Bradshaw in 1877. There was little change over the horse-drawn period, but Herber Toll Gate disappeared from the timetables in 1881; the toll-house was in the angle between the main line and the Herber Siding.

By 1884 the GVT Co. was regretting it had taken over the management of the line and there was a general wish that the Shropshire Union Canal Co.

The tramway from Black Park Bottom Wharf (*top left*) through Chirk station to Pontfaen: from the 6 inch Ordnance Survey of Shropshire, 1902. *Courtesy Ordnance Survey*

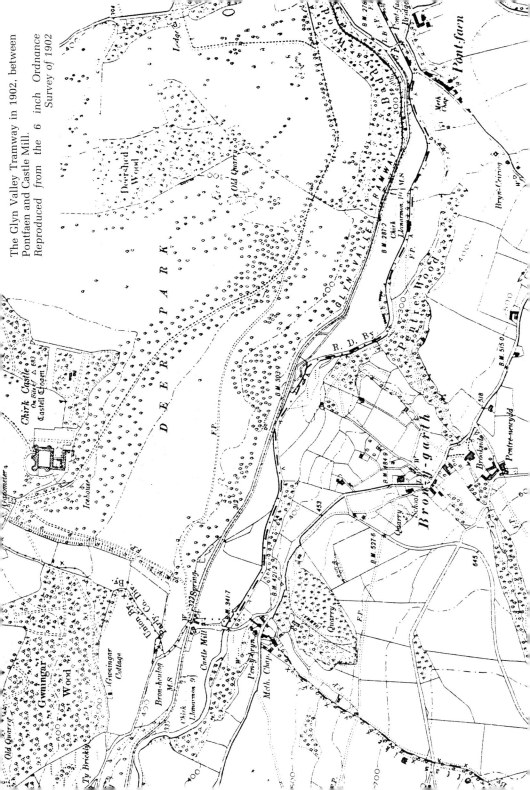

The Glyn Valley Tramway in 1902, between Pontfaen and Castle Mill. Reproduced from the 6 inch Ordnance Survey of 1902

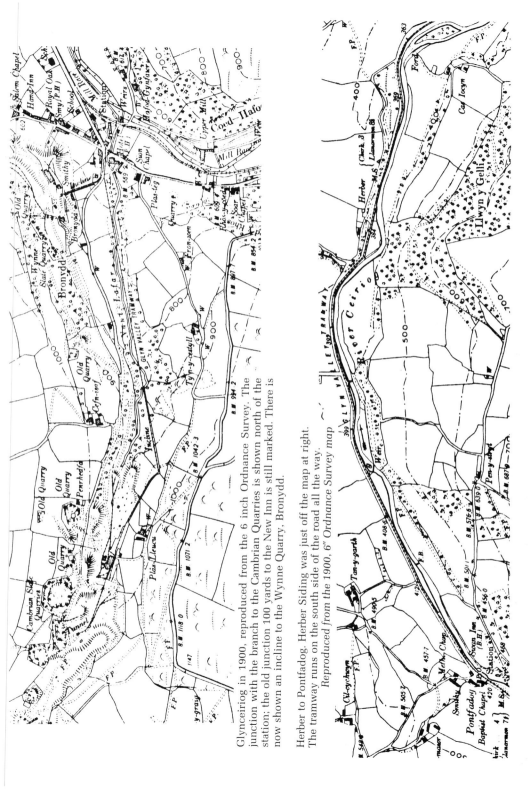

Glynceiriog in 1900, reproduced from the 6 inch Ordnance Survey. The junction with the branch to the Cambrian Quarries is shown north of the station; the old junction 100 yards to the New Inn is still marked. There is now shown an incline to the Wynne Quarry, Bronydd.

Herber to Pontfadog. Herber Siding was just off the map at right. The tramway runs on the south side of the road all the way. Reproduced from the 1900, 6" Ordnance Survey map

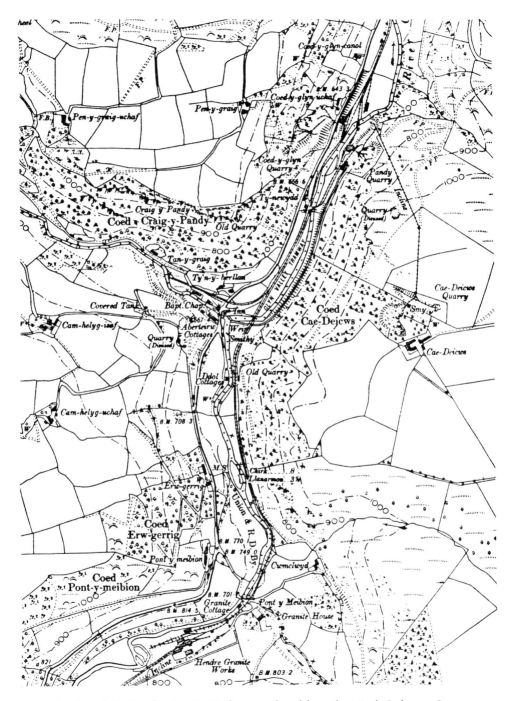

Pandy and the Hendre Granite Works, reproduced from the 6 inch Ordnance Survey of 1900. Note the short spur line up the side valley at Pandy. From the bottom of the map tracks continue a few hundred yards into the quarries.

Courtesy Ordnance Survey

should work it once again. The canal company, not unnaturally, expressed complete lack of interest. The inevitable action, if the line was not to decay slowly, was at last taken by the Board of Directors of the GVT Co., and a Parliamentary Bill was prepared in early 1885 to convert the line to steam traction. Apart from the compelling nature of the situation, this was a somewhat belated decision, taking the history of Welsh slate railways as a whole. The Penrhyn Quarries in North Wales had been operating a horse-tramway to the Menai Straits as early as 1801, and turned to steam in 1876. The dates for the Blaenau Festiniog quarries were respectively 1836 and 1863, and the Padarn quarries at Llanberis 1824 and 1848. The owner of the Bryneglwys quarry at Abergynolwen started to build a six-mile steam-worked line to Tywyn as soon as he was confident of the approaching main-line railway being built, and opened it in 1866. The Corris, Machynlleth & River Dovey Tramroad, opened with horse-haulage in 1859, was similar to the Glyn Valley in many ways, being almost entirely a roadside line, but the Act under which it was later authorised to operate steam trains did not require it to observe the usual tramway restrictions. Only one major slate tramway of the era never progressed from horse to steam; this was the 1860 line from the Croesor Valley down to Portmadoc; the probable reason was that the upper half of the line continued only by a series of gravity inclines. From 1923 its lower half was worked by the Welsh Highland Railway by steam.

In addition to the above examples, Dennis himself had surveyed a narrow gauge steam railway not far away, the Snailbeach Railway opened in 1877. This had a fearsome gradient from a reversing station at Snailbeach to the Stiperstones Mine, which must have reminded him of that from Pontfaen eastwards on the original Glyn Valley line.

The Bill contained all the desired features and met with no obstruction from Col Biddulph when it came to the matter of taking the line up the northern hillside to reach the GWR at Chirk. The new route moved across the road to the north side at Pontfaen and then ascended into Baddy's Wood on a gradient of 1 in 40 for a short distance, rejoining the line of the road but at a higher level, before crossing the drive to the Castle Deer park to swing north, on top of the tunnel containing the canal, to Chirk station.

A prospectus of 1885 states that 'at the time the line was constructed (1873), the consent of the owner of the land could not be obtained' for a northern approach and then adds that agreement had been reached with Col Biddulph to construct a new line to connect with the GWR and the SUC at Chirk 'for its entire distance through his land upon most favourable terms; this removes the real impediment to the success of the existing undertaking'. What occasioned a change of heart in the Colonel is not known, but as he had an interest in the granite quarry at Hendre he may have felt he was cutting off his nose to spite his face.

The Bill emerged as the Glyn Valley Tramway Act, 1885, authorising the new Chirk routing, the extension to Tregeiriog and the use of steam power. Minor points included the authorisation of short deviations at Dolywern and Glyn to avoid sharp curves, the necessity to carry HM Mail if required to do so by the Postmaster-General and a three-year completion period.

Glyn Valley Tramway

All eager to be captured on film, this early view of *Sir Theodore* at Glynceiriog station shows the tramway well used.

Courtesy Heyday Publishing

The Bill had included a provision for a connection at Chirk to the Shropshire Union Canal. Although an earlier proposal by Dennis had included a tramway across Chirk Aqueduct to a wharf at Chirk Bank, this would in fact have been very difficult, and in the new circumstances it was decided to join the canal north of the aqueduct, and the obvious place was Black Park Bottom Wharf, where there was a double cut into the east bank for boat mooring. This would involve the GVT extension tramway passing under the GWR (it was already now on the east side of the canal). This it did 250 yards north of the point where the Black Park branch railway left the GWR main line, and ran alongside the southernmost canal wharf on its north side. This was known as the Bottom Wharf, as the siding off the Black Park line serving road transport off the Holyhead Road had always been known as the Top Wharf, though there was no canal there.

A further provision of the Bill resulted from the strong protest by J.R. Barnes, owner of the Quinta Estate, against the closure of the tramway to Pontfaen. His lessee David Lomax claimed that 90 per cent of his traffic went to the GVT, though this perhaps represented only a proportion of the traffic that did not go to the GWR. In any case, the Parliamentary Committee accepted his plea that his colliery would be entirely cut off, and laid down that the tramway to Pontfaen must remain in place, that the GVT must supply wagons for taking coal to the new canal terminal at Chirk, and that Trehowell Colliery should receive a 3d. per ton rebate on traffic passing up the valley to Glyn. These were onerous terms, but fortunately for the GVT, the colliery which had produced some 250 tons of coal per day in 1884 was down to 50 tons in 1885, the coal seam having turned out to be less productive than expected. The tramway between the GWR bridge and Pontfaen was to cease to be a public carrier, and became in effect an extension of Barnes's private railway from Trehowell to the bridge; it is doubtful whether it was much used.

It was estimated that the cost of re-building the tramway for steam traction would amount to £15,165 of which the Chirk route absorbed £3,559 and the Tregeiriog extension £5,034. The purchase of two locomotives and new rolling stock was estimated to cost another £3,000. This meant that just over £18,000 capital had to be found. The Directors confidently explained that 80,000 tons of down traffic and 10,000 tons of up traffic would be secured each year and that this would secure a 10 per cent dividend on the new total authorised capital of £38,020 which took the form of 3,802 £10 shares. Of this sum at that time £12,926 represented paid-up capital and liabilities. By May 1886 the necessary capital had been subscribed and the Shropshire Union Canal Co. had sold its £6,000 worth of shares to the GVT Co. for £2,400. The financial and final link with the canal company had been broken.

Robert Stewart, of a London firm, who had surveyed the line and prepared the plans, was appointed Engineer for the construction and Mr H. Croom-Johnson of Wrexham was the contractor.

Henry Dennis, at the time of the conversion, was also the Engineer of the Snailbeach District Railway, already mentioned, worked by steam on the unique gauge of 2 ft 4 in. It had fallen on lean times in 1887 when the GVT

was about to be converted to steam traction and in consequence Dennis
hired both the Snailbeach locomotives to Croom-Johnson as contractors'
engines.

The two engines in question were *Belmont*, an 0–4–2ST built by Hughes
of Loughborough, and *Fernhill*, an 0–6–0ST, the builder of which is not
known. At one time it was believed to have been built by Stephen Lewin of
Poole, but a recent definitive book on this builder makes that unlikely. Both
returned to Snailbeach at the end of the contract.

It is these locomotives which probably altered the GVT gauge by a quarter
of an inch from 2 ft 4¼ in. to 2 ft 4½ in. As late as 1933 the Secretary of the
company was still describing the gauge in official correspondence as
2 ft 4¼ in. but in fact it had been 2 ft 4½ in. ever since the conversion to
steam in 1888 despite the fact that the authorising Act specified there was to
be no change in the gauge. On their own line the 2 ft 4 in. gauge Snailbeach
locomotives followed a fairly straight track without severe curves, but no
doubt on starting to work on the Glyn Valley line, which closely followed all
the twists and turns of the turnpike road, it was found that their wheel
flanges were distorting the track on sharp curves and opening out the gauge.
This is thought to be the most likely explanation for the adoption of a gauge
which was, and is, found nowhere else in the British Isles.

The work of conversion started at Pontfaen in the early spring of 1887,
with the two Snailbeach locomotives, *Belmont* and *Fernhill* being delivered
by road from Chirk station. A long siding was laid at Pontfaen north of the
river, at the end of which was an engine shed to take the two locomotives.
Two gangs worked outwards from this point, one relaying the existing
tramway with 50 lb./yd rails, whilst the other cut the new approach to Chirk.
This track rose at 1 in 64 for three-quarters of a mile, and at the summit there
was a small cutting. The old rails lifted from the section west of Pontfaen
were sold to the Kerry Tramway in Montgomeryshire. This was a 2 ft gauge
railway 5 miles long laid in 1888 by C.J. Naylor to connect his woodlands
and timber-mills with the terminus of the Kerry branch of the Cambrian
Railways from Abermule. It was locomotive-worked, but as the engine
weighed less than 4 tons the horse-tram rails were adequate. When Mr
Naylor moved on in 1895 the rails were taken up and sold to a dealer in
Derby, and may well have seen further use.

Although the GVT had ceased to carry passengers in 1886, it continued to
handle mineral traffic during the process of conversion, difficult though that
may have been. The 16-year old timekeeper to the contractor was a Thomas
Griffiths, who in his 75th year in 1946 recollected some aspects of the work,
and wrote, 'I remember a few scraps and scrapes among the navvies,
especially in wet weather when they would go to the "fuddle." Once they
were working near Pontfadog and went on the spree at the Swan Inn where
several slept overnight in the coal-house and next morning turned out to
work as black as the devil.'

Unfortunately, the 'scraps and scrapes' were also occurring in the Boardroom. There was some trouble over the purchase of the shares remaining
with the canal company, which led on, as these things do, to a confrontation

at the General Meeting in June 1888. This resulted in the Chairman, R. Biddulph, resigning from the Board. The company's finances were also in a bad way, and the friction at the top did not help in raising more money locally; during this period the remaining Directors had to dip into their own pockets. This was not undeserved; they had not managed affairs very well.

As the line had to be working by the 31st July, 1888 (Parliamentary grace), the work went on apace. At Chirk the line ran beside the main line railway to the GWR station where transfer sidings for mineral traffic and the company's headquarters were to be built. The new line then accompanied the GWR line for three-quarters of a mile to gain access to the canal at the two-fingered basin which worked the Black Park Colliery traffic. At Glynceiriog the new extension left the road and followed the bottom of the valley beside the Ceiriog river on its own private right of way, going only as far as the Hendre granite quarry and not to the village of Tregeiriog another mile beyond, as authorised. In this section the gradient was more severe than that encountered below Glynceiriog and averaged about 1 in 65.

The eventual and total expenditure on the GVT between 1870 and 1895 to make it into an operating concern was £63,661 or about £7,300 per mile. Comparative sums for the Talyllyn, Snailbeach and Festiniog Railways were £2,150, £6,150 and £10,750 respectively.

The steam conversion year of 1888 also marked, by a coincidence, the removal of all tolls on turnpike roads in the area and the placing of the Denbighshire part of the Wem and Bronygarth Turnpike in the hands of the newly created Denbighshire County Council.

Yet another posed photograph on the Hendre extension just beyond Glynceiriog station was taken by Burns, a local photographer. The caption was changed on postcards after 1935 to 'The Late Glyn Valley Train'; the engine is *Sir Theodore*.

Author's Collection

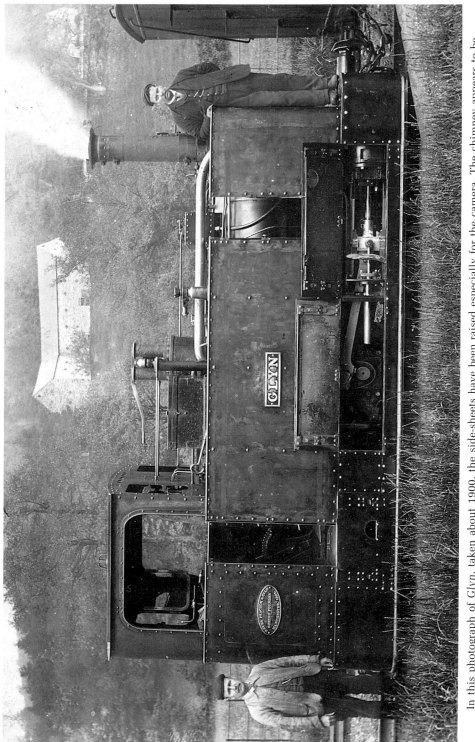

In this photograph of *Glyn*, taken about 1900, the side-sheets have been raised especially for the camera. The chimney appears to be patched in three places, probably due to an accident.

Locomotive Publishing Co.

The Steam Railway – Tram Locomotives and Rolling Stock

The line was physically ready to carry mineral traffic by July 1888, although there were many details, especially at the railway and canal termini at Chirk, which had not been completed. Board of Trade Inspectors had visited the line in March 1887 and they came again in October 1888, but advised that the work was too incomplete to issue a certificate. A further inspection was made in July 1889, which resulted again in a certificate being withheld until certain lengths of the line had iron railings erected to protect the public. The company was in two minds; it needed more traffic, yet hesitated to hasten the re-opening as money was owed on several items of plant, including one engine, and re-opening to passengers would require expenditure on carriages.

Two engines had however been ordered, from Beyer Peacock of Manchester. The first, *Sir Theodore*, was delivered on 17th October, 1888; it was named after the Chairman of the company, Sir Theodore Martin, K.C.B., K.C.V.O. (1816–1909), who at this time was 73 years of age.

He was no local squire but a man of some talent. As a parliamentary agent and solicitor at Westminster, he had prepared and piloted successfully through the committee stage many a private Bill including those relating to the Shrewsbury and Chester Railway and the River Dee Navigation. He knew the Ceiriog Valley well, for he had also dealt with the Wem and Bronygarth Road and GVT Bills. Furthermore he owned the ground rights of the land occupied by the Cambrian slate quarries. His profession was but part of his life for he was deeply interested in art, literature, music and drama. Because of his knowledge of German and his literary facility he was invited by Queen Victoria, who had never met him, to write the official biography of the Prince Consort. This he did in a span of 12 years and became a close friend of the Queen in the process, receiving as his reward a knighthood in 1878.

The locomotive *Sir Theodore* was joined in April 1889 by a twin sister engine, *Dennis*, named after Henry Dennis, who was now also a Director of the company. It is presumed that at this stage, or late 1888, the Snailbeach engines were withdrawn and returned to their home lines.

The Board of Trade Railway Returns first record the GVT in the last quarter of 1888 and show that 6,013 tons of minerals were carried and 2,400 train miles worked in three months. This represents two round trips per day except for a single trip on Saturdays. In the first complete year, 1889, the train mileage pattern was maintained but pro-rata the tonnage dropped by half, totalling 13,795 tons. Two-thirds of this was down traffic, mostly granite, whilst about 4,750 tons were up transhipments from the Shropshire Union Canal at Black Park Basin. This up traffic probably consisted of coal, lime and bricks which were available for the first time in quantity at comparatively cheap rates. Very little down traffic is recorded for canal transhipment so the bulk of it must have been going into standard gauge railway wagons at Chirk station (GWR).

The next three years showed considerable and progressive increases in the tonnages carried by the line, namely: 1890 – 20,325 tons, 1891 – 28,039 tons, 1892 – 49,022 tons. The line's traffic-carrying potential gave confidence to the slate quarry owners, and in 1890 slate mining was introduced for the first time in the Ceiriog Valley when the Wynne Quarry at Glynceiriog was converted from open face to mine working. This decision was well rewarded, for the 1890 slate production of 1,275 tons was about doubled by 1893.

The success of the introduction of steam locomotives in hauling and stimulating the growth of mineral traffic, and the pleas of those living in the upper part of the valley, induced the company to introduce passenger services between Chirk and Glynceiriog at the beginning of the 1890s. Two stations, in the proper sense of the word, were built at the termini complete with platforms and red brick offices, the one at Chirk adjoining the down GWR platform. Two intermediate 'stations' were also built at Pontfadog and Dolywern, each consisting of a small building holding a waiting room and office and no platform. Pontfadog station lay on the opposite side of the road to the line whilst at Dolywern it was sited on the deviation on the company's property.

There seems to have been some sort of passenger traffic in the summer of 1890; there was at least one closed carriage, and a rough open one, from the horse-tram days. At some time before March 1891 the first carriage had come from the Midland Railway Carriage & Wagon Co. at Shrewsbury. This was an odd vehicle, with a centre door and a low clerestory roof; it seems probable that it was something left on the makers' hands – the GVT had left the ordering of passenger stock very late, perhaps because it could not afford it.

Regular passenger traffic started on Monday 15th March, 1891, and was operated without a break, except for the general railway strike in 1926, until its abandonment on Saturday 1st April, 1933. Passenger traffic beyond Glynceiriog was limited to quarrymen's trains and specials which were never advertised.

The opening day for steam hauled passenger trains was a gala occasion for the valley despite the fact it had had a tramway for 18 years and steam traction for three years. Not much fuss was made of the first train of the day which left Chirk at 6.55 am, but the 2.00 pm was accorded the honours. It left Chirk in a blaze of detonating fog signals and was met at Pontfadog by the Glynceiriog Brass Band. By this time there was no room on the train and the musicians had to be accommodated in some wagons hastily attached to the rear. The local paper reported in a kindly fashion, not stressing that the train's capacity was about 30 persons, being more interested in the fact that the horses passed did not seem distressed by the engine. It must have been quite a cheerful occasion for the Board also, for there was the prospect of considerable traffic from new roadstone and chinastone deposits at Pandy.

The introduction of passenger services placed a considerable load on the two engines and a further locomotive of the same design was purchased to give them relief. This was named Glyn and she entered service in May 1892.

The locomotives of the tramway had a distinctive box-like appearance;

A good view of the Baldwin standing on the Hendre extension at Glynceiriog in May 1932.   *H.C. Casserley*

The coal yard at Glynceiriog, with *Glyn* on duty in the foreground, photographed around 1930.   *Lens of Sutton*

their shape was due to a schedule of design requirements laid down in the 1885 Act which stipulated that every engine was to have:

(a) Such mechanical appliances for preventing its motive power from operating and for bringing it, and any carriage drawn or propelled by such engine, to a stand.

(b) Freedom from noise produced by blast or clatter of machinery; such machinery to be concealed from view at all parts above four inches from the level of the rails; all fire to be concealed from view.

(c) An indicator by means of which its speed shall be shown.

(d) Suitable fender to push aside obstructions.

(e) A special bell, whistle or other apparatus as a warning.

(f) A seat for the driver so placed in front of such engine as to command the fullest possible view of the road before him.

(g) A speed not exceeding eight miles per hour.

This schedule was not specifically designed for the Glyn Valley Tramway but was copied from the requirements laid down for street tramways. Steam locomotives running on rails on a public road were viewed with mistrust, for at that time all road traffic was horse drawn and public opinion held that such engines would frighten horses and cause accidents. In consequence, Parliament introduced very stringent regulations for the design and operation of street tramway locomotives in the Use of Mechanical Power on Tramways Act, 1879. Basically, it called for a locomotive showing no fire, steam , smoke or moving parts and moving at a speed not exceeding 10 miles per hour with the minimum of noise.

British locomotive-builders were not without some experience of the kind of engine required. The first steam tram engines had been run in Leicester in 1876, but the first large-scale use was in Leeds in 1878, with a design by Kitsons, running on four wheels, totally enclosed and having condensing gear and facilities for being driven from either end. Later the Wilkinson design of engine, gear-driven and with a vertical boiler, was built by Beyer Peacock, Green, Falcon and others. Although some town tramways were of less than standard gauge, none was as narrow as the Glyn Valley. To consider the practice on true road-side narrow gauge railways, one must look at Ireland, which was at that time subject to the same by-laws as the rest of the British Isles. All were of 3 ft gauge. The first two, the Giants Causeway Tramway in 1883 and Portstewart Tramway in 1882, used scaled-down conventional tram engines, respectively by Wilkinsons and Kitsons. Totally-enclosed four-wheelers were also adopted by the Castlederg & Victoria Bridge, 1883, (by Kitson), and Schull & Skibbereen, 1886, (by Dick Kerr). However, later lines discarded this type; the Cork & Muskerry in 1887 used Falcon 2−4−0T engines with skirting only, and the Clogher Valley Railway the same year purchased Sharp, Stewart 0−4−2T engines, also only with skirting below the running plate. These were very similar to the Beyer Peacock design for the Glyn Valley locomotives.

The Manchester firm of Beyer Peacock and Co. Ltd was established in 1854 to build both standard and narrow gauge locomotives and it was one of about half a dozen companies which decided to enter the steam tram market. Between 1881 and 1886 it built 71 patented steam tram engines with vertical

Drawing illustrating the first two locomotives.   *Courtesy Model Railway News*

boilers and followed these by another 16, for tramways in Birmingham and Manchester, to its own design with horizontal boilers.

The three engines, *Sir Theodore*, *Dennis* and *Glyn*, cost £1,200 each and were 0–4–2 side tank engines weighing 14½ tons in working order and in design were nearer to being railway locomotives than street tramway engines, though their parentage was never in doubt. They had a different wheel arrangement, and were bigger and more powerful than British street tramway engines, and did not have duplicated controls at both ends of the locomotive. They had four coupled driving wheels and what was in practice a leading set of carrying wheels, for there was the legal requirement that engines must be worked cab first. Conventionally rated 0–4–2s, it might be less misleading to describe them as 2–4–0s.

Despite these obvious differences, the schedule at the beginning of the Glyn Valley Tramway Act 1885, ensured that they had several tram engine characteristics. They were fired with coke, though in later years coal was substituted, had a condensing apparatus for the exhaust steam, were completely enclosed above rail level, and were fitted with both whistle and bell. The condensing apparatus consisted of taking used steam from the cylinders into the water tanks, but this so over-heated the water that the system was quickly abandoned and the fitments removed in 1921. Steam governors were fitted to each engine and were connected to a pointer moving over a dial to provide a crude form of speedometer. The governors shut off the steam supply when a speed of 10 mph was exceeded.

Sir Theodore and *Dennis* had boilers with 75 tubes working to a pressure of 150 lb. per square inch. These boilers had flat topped steam domes containing a regulator and were surmounted by Ramsbottom safety valves, which in turn were flanked by an injector and whistle respectively, and were mounted on outside frames which were carried on six laminated springs bearing upon the three axles. The side casing above footplate height had a door, sited just to the rear of the smoke box, to give access to areas about the boiler, and below the frame there were three hinged sections to allow for the oiling and inspection of the motion.

The locomotives were driven from the left-hand side of the footplate where the driver had the use of two rear cab windows for his forward driving view. These were glazed and could be opened. The footplate controls were conventionally sited and above the driver on the cab roof was a hand bell. The fireman obtained coal from a bunker at the rear of the cab, and sand was held in a container above the fire box. Fitments included central buffing irons, single link and hook couplings, carriage side chains at the chimney end only, and front and rear lamp brackets sited 7 ft above rail level. A tool box and lifting jack were always carried on the top of the right-hand water tank.

Three lessons were quickly learnt about the design and working of these two engines and were incorporated in the design of *Glyn*, which was built two years later. She had her frame length increased by one foot to give more bunker and footplate space in the cab, and the cab itself was totally enclosed. The two earlier engines had the chimney side of their cabs cut away, which gave inadequate protection in driving rain, and soon had

The Baldwin in 1932 showing clearly the livery and lining out.   *H.C. Casserley*

A rear view of the Baldwin just after the sale, seen here inside the engine shed.
                                                                            Lens of Sutton

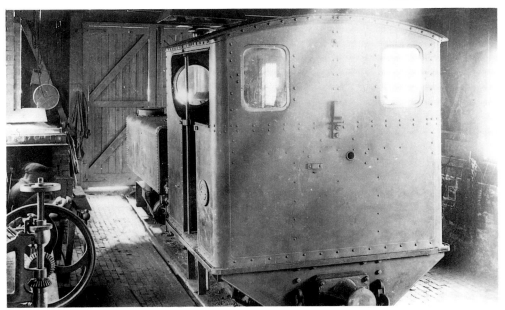

portable screens fitted which were only removed on hot summer days. The sanding arrangements had been found to be inadequate and an additional box was mounted on the forward part of the boiler top. Sir Theodore and Dennis were modified in this latter respect.

At a distance the 'twins' and Glyn could be differentiated by two small but distinctive features. Glyn carried her maker's name on the casing to the rear of the cab door whereas the twins had theirs forward of the front inspection door. Secondly, Sir Theodore and Dennis had two sand-pots mounted on the running plate in the front of the smoke box door, a feature absent in Glyn. Details of the fourth locomotive to be acquired by the GVT in 1921, are given at the end of the chapter. It is believed that the third engine, Glyn, was delivered with sprung buffers, and that the solid buffers of the first two were modified. In general however there was no major change to these engines in their lifetime, apart from the removal of the condensing gear in 1921.

Dimensions of the Beyer Peacock Engines

Overall length	18 ft 8 in. (Glyn 19 ft 8 in.)
Overall width	6 ft 7 in.
Overall height	9 ft 6 in.
Wheelbase	9 ft 3 in., coupled 4 ft 3 in.
Wheel diameter – driving and leading	2 ft 6 in. and 1 ft 9 in.
Grate area	6.5 square feet
Total heating surface	261 square feet
Tubes	75 by $1\frac{5}{8}$ in. o.d. brass
Boiler pressure	150 lb. p.s.i.
Cylinders	$10\frac{1}{2}$ in. by 16 in.
Tractive effort at:	
75% boiler pressure	6.620 lb.
85% boiler pressure	7,500 lb.
Water tanks	340 gallons
Bunkerage	7 cwt.
Weight: empty	12 tons 11 cwt.
working	14 tons 11 cwt.

After World War I the mechanical state of the three locomotives was not good. They had been working for some 30 years and collectively had run over one million miles, of which 70 per cent were train miles and 30 per cent shunting miles. In consequence at least one engine (name unknown) needed drastic overhaul and so the company went shopping for another locomotive. In 1920 the Disposal Board of the Ministry of Munitions was selling much railway material and so it came about that a 60 cm. gauge locomotive of the Light Railway Operating Division (LROD) of the Corps of Royal Engineers became GVT property.

In France in World War I there developed a 60 cm. gauge (1 ft 11⅝ in.) system of military light railways on the British front which connected the standard gauge railheads with the rear trenches. At first man and animal power was used but in late 1916 it was decided to mechanise the system by using steam locomotives between the railheads and the point where steam and smoke would draw the enemy's artillery fire, and electric and i.c.

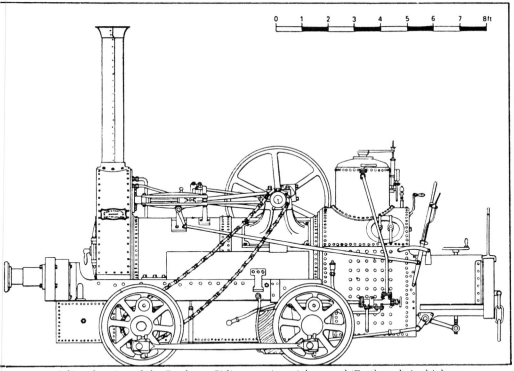

A line drawing of the Boultons Sidings engine nick-named 'Rattlesnake' which was purchased by the Trehowell Colliery in 1884 and may have worked the joint Trehowell/GVT exchange siding at Preesgwyn. *Courtesy Oakwood Press*

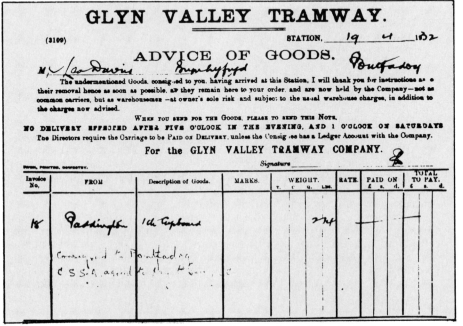

An advice of goods form sent to the author's father in 1932.

tractors in the forward areas. Britain turned to the United States for help and placed an order for some 500 4−6−0 side tank engines with the Baldwin Locomotive Company of Philadelphia; this order accounted for 75 per cent of all the steam locomotives to be used on the system. All the Baldwin engines were of identical design and were built for a short and hectic life with inadequate maintenance, and few survived to do a peacetime job. They were shipped to the U.K. in pieces, mainly in early 1917, and most of them worked on the Western Front, though a few were used behind the fighting lines in Italy, Greece and Palestine.

The engine that the GVT purchased had the Baldwin works number 45221 which indicates she was one of the last of the WD order to be completed; it is thought she was allocated the LROD No. 1089 which was subsequently changed to 639. She had arrived in France by August 1917 and nothing is known of her whereabouts until September 1919 when she lay, with some 250 of her sisters, at a dump at Purfleet, Essex. In a sale catalogue dated November 1919 a number of engines of this class were described as 'practically new' but it is not known if this applied to No. 45221. She was delivered carrying LROD No. 1089.

The GVT's acquisition was typically American in appearance, with two domes surmounting the boiler, the first holding sand. The steam dome was surmounted by two pop safety valves and whistle. The engine weighed 14½ tons in working order, had bar frames and outside cylinders with square cased slide valves and Walschaerts gear. She was sent to Beyer Peacock Ltd in January 1921 for alterations and conversion to the 2 ft 4½ in. gauge. The frames were widened with packing pieces between the cylinders; the utilitarian appearance of the locomotive was softened by capping the stove-pipe chimney and removing its top damper and by closing in the open rear cab. The two large acetylene lamps, cab spectacle shades and suction hose (for replenishing tanks from streams and shell holes) were removed and the swivelling buffing irons were replaced with fixed ones of GVT pattern. Carriage side chains were added at both ends. The locomotive was painted black, lined-out and had the letters 'G.V.T.' painted on her side tanks. This foreign locomotive was never numbered or named but was simply referred to as 'Baldwin' and could always be detected by her haunting chime whistle, which conjured up visions for me as a boy of buffalo, the Middle West and Red Indians. The purchase and conversion cost about £3,000.

'Baldwin' was less powerful than the tram engines and was considered by crews to be rather a rough rider. In consequence, she worked mineral trains only whenever possible. Like all members of her class, she was an indifferent steamer and had to have her tubes well cleaned at all times and could suffer from clogged injectors because these were of very small design. In mitigation it must be said that 'Baldwin' worked her fair share of the traffic and, having been designed for a short and rough life over temporarily laid lines, she did well to put in another 15 years of useful work. She was set to work facing Glynceiriog and remained like this always as the turntables were too short for her 12 ft 4 in. wheelbase.

The GVT was not the only line to acquire such a type of locomotive, though it was the only one to smarten up the appearance of its purchase. The

Snailbeach Railway purchased two and the West Highland Railway, Ashover Light Railway in Derbyshire and Associated Portland Cement Co. Ltd purchased another eight between them. 'Baldwin' must have brought relief to the hard pressed tram engines for one, or all three in turn, were shown as unserviceable between and including 1921 and 1925. Heavy repairs undertaken by contractors are shown as two in 1921 and one each in 1924 and 1927. These were performed either by Beyer Peacock Ltd or by two small Wrexham firms called Cudworth and Johnson, and Curtiss. It is known that Cudworth and Johnson re-tubed *Sir Theodore* in 1921 and the 'Baldwin' at a later date. On this latter job the firm apparently made little profit for they failed to recover the value of the scrap brass tubes; these tubes on withdrawal were found to be made of steel capped with brass ferrules!

Dimensions of the Baldwin

Overall length	19 ft 6 in.
Overall width	6 ft 6 in.
Overall height	9 ft 3 in.
Wheelbase	12 ft 4 in., coupled 5 ft 10 in.
Wheel diameter (driving)	1 ft 11½ in.
Wheel diameter (leading)	1 ft 4 in.
Grate area	5.6 square feet
Total heating surface	254½ square feet
Tubes	83 by 1½ in. o.d. steel
Boiler pressure	178 lb. p.s.i.
Cylinders	9 in. by 12 in.
Tractive effort (75% BP)	5,510 lb.
Tractive effort (85% BP)	6,260 lb.
Water tanks	396 gallons
Bunkerage	15¾ cwt.
Weight empty	10 tons 15 cwt.
Weight working	14 tons 10 cwt.

With the Baldwin in service, the opportunity was taken to send *Sir Theodore* back to Beyer Peacock for a major overhaul. The order for the work was made out in 1920, but it was four years before it was put in hand. Apart from a new boiler, some smaller alterations were made as a result of experience, including moving the brake cylinder to the other side, taking away the remains of the disused condensing gear and fitting new trailing axle springs. The scrapping 12 years later of an engine in such excellent condition must be painful indeed to the modern narrow-gauge preservationist.

The passenger carriages in horse-drawn days comprised three only, one open and the others closed; one of the latter had two compartments fully glazed, but was considerably narrower than later carriages. The open one was normally covered by an awning held by stanchions. The single horse was not in shafts, but attached by long straps from the collar to the drawbar. This was the usual system with town trams, though the pioneer rural horse-tramway, the Swansea & Mumbles, had always used shafts. The danger of over-running the horse when stopping was not great bearing in mind the slow pace. To what extent horses were used in tandem is not known; on

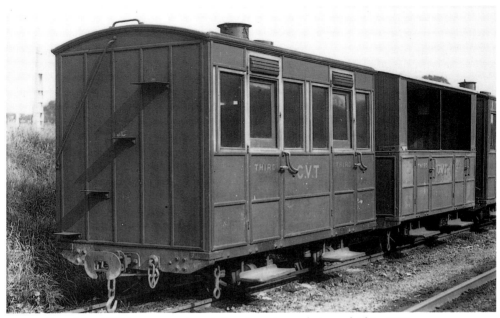

One of the 1893 two-compartment closed carriages photographed in 1932.

H.C. Casserley

Two centre-door Thirds at Chirk in 1932; note that the second (clerestory) vehicle, which was the first carriage delivered, has had a 'stable door' fitted, the part above it being a sliding window.

H.C. Casserley

town tramways often a lead horse was attached for hills. The closed coaches ended up as huts, one at Hand Lane bridge, Chirk, the other at Castle Mill. The closed van is believed to have been similarly used in Chirk sidings.

The stock figures shown in the 'Railway Returns' indicate that the GVT built up its steam traction rolling stock between 1888 and 1893, after which later date only minor additions were made.

The rolling stock order for carriages, wagons and vans was put in hand with the Midland Railway Carriage and Wagon Co. Ltd, Shrewsbury. This company, which had no connection with the Midland Railway, built and repaired all types of rolling stock for railways and street tramways. Its activities in Shrewsbury ceased just before World War I, when it was absorbed into what is now the Metropolitan-Cammell Carriage and Wagon Co. Ltd. The Midland Co. produced design drawings for an 'Open Wagon,' 'Third Class Car,' 'First Class Car,' 'Open Car' and 'Covered Wagon' which are still in existence.

Two, or possibly three, carriages were delivered in 1891: a centre-door 3rd saloon with clerestory roof, and another centre-door saloon with a flat roof; an open two-compartment carriage, somewhat narrower than the others, may have come from Midland at this time, or perhaps a few years later.

Nine more carriages came from the same maker in 1893: six open cars (later given roofs and boarded ends) and two 2-compartment closed thirds. There was also a 'first', which was similar to the thirds but furnished inside to a higher standard and carried on leaf springs instead of coil springs.

The thirds carried 16 passengers and the first 12.

The 'clerestore' coach appeared in the 1905 catalogue of W.G. Bagnall & Co. Ltd, with other vehicles showing the types available and their prices; it had 'Workmens Carriage' painted on the side, but whether this was ever done is doubtful. Two of the 2-compartment thirds were also later allocated to workmen; this was commonly done on railways at the time because of the amount of dust on the clothes of miners and quarrymen.

By 1894 the GVT owned 12 coaches and 238 wagons and vans, and the peak was reached in 1901 when four new coaches (probably two open and two closed) and 20 mineral wagons (total cost £790) were added to the existing stock. At the same time two of the oldest coaches were withdrawn. This made a grand total of 14 coaches and 258 other vehicles.

The four closed 3rds of 'standard' pattern were quite cosy affairs with two compartments, upholstered seats, window blinds, central oil lamp and roof ventilator and the fifth, or 1st class, coach went one better by having luggage racks, mirrors, and gilt mouldings. The author can recollect, as a boy in 1932, travelling in one of these closed coaches on a winter's night and still remembers the fug compounded of lamp oil, tobacco smoke and manure-stained clothing! Externally these five closed coaches were of similar appearance. Each had two doors on each side with individual steps, and at one end four step irons and handrail to gain access to the roof and at the other a parking hand brake. On the roof was a single ventilated lamp pot.

The six open coaches were of the same dimensions, door arrangement and seating plan as the closed ones described above, but had waist high sides

The guard's vans, one of which is seen here at Chirk, had a compartment at the end which was used to issue tickets, especially at halts en route.   *Lens of Sutton*

One of the two carriages rebuilt by the Talyllyn Railway. It is run as First Class No. 14; said to have also been GVT No. 14, seen here at Dolgoch on 27th June, 1972. *D. Gould*

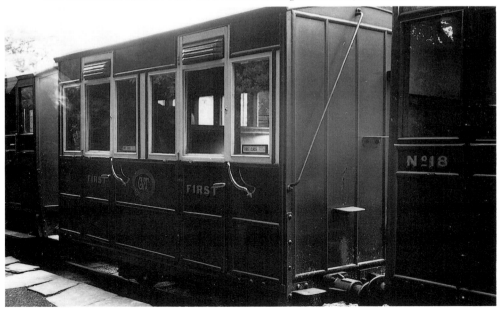

only and roofs supported by six iron stanchions; about 1910 wooden end screens were fitted. These closed and open coaches cost the modest sums of £88 and £60 apiece, respectively.

There were two 'oddities': the clerestory saloon already mentioned, which as a new coach was used in the inaugural passenger train in March, 1891. (Newspaper quote: 'One of the new coaches, used on Monday, together with one of the old ones and an open car, was manufactured by the Midland Carriage Co.'.) The remaining 'odd' coach, an open one, was longer and narrower than the rest of the coaching stock (4 ft 6 in. wide) and had a vaguely continental look. Entry to this was not by the usual compartment door but by open platforms at each end of the vehicle, and for small boys there was the added attraction of a screw hand brake which could be manipulated, unnoticed by the crew, when the train was moving.

Irrespective of design, all carriages were fitted with central buffers, two types of couplings and sets of side chains, of identical pattern. The buffers had an aperture through which a coupling bar, with an eye at each end, was passed and secured by dropping a pin through the eye behind the buffer head. The spare coupling bars were hung under the coach corners when not in use. This method of coupling was only effected between carriages and the more conventional link and hook was used with locomotives and goods vehicles. Steps were provided only on the north or road side of all the carriages.

All the carriages except the 'oddities' had an outside body width of 5 ft 10 in.; those of the closed carriages were 11 ft 7 in. long and the open ones two inches longer. The wheelbase in all cases was 5 ft 6 in.

The carriages were painted medium green with elaborate gold lining-out; the GVT monogram (later gartered crest) was placed on the centre panels.

Two vehicles which were in effect passenger stock were the brake vans Nos. 3 and 4, which had a compartment at one end from which the guard issued tickets, and which were invariably found on any train, though sometimes there would be some wagons between the carriages and the van. These came from the Birmingham Carriage & Wagon Co. and were ordered in 1889. The bodies were 10½ ft long, width 5½ ft and wheel base 4 ft 10 in. There was a 2 ft wide door opening onto the 'verandah' and another similar one leading into the body itself, which contained a ticket press. Screw brake, coke stove, sprung central buffers and lamp brackets at four corners were fitted.

Dimensions of 'Standard' Coach

	ft	in.		ft	in.
Length	14	3	Height	9	6
(frame)	11	7	(internal)	6	5½
(internal)	11	1	Floor level	2	0
Width	6	11	Wheel diameter	1	8
(frame)	5	10	Wheelbase	5	6
(internal)	5	4			

A goods van coupled to one of the early 2 ton wagons. *Lens of Sutton*

The narrow open saloon, photographed in 1932. *H.C. Casserley*

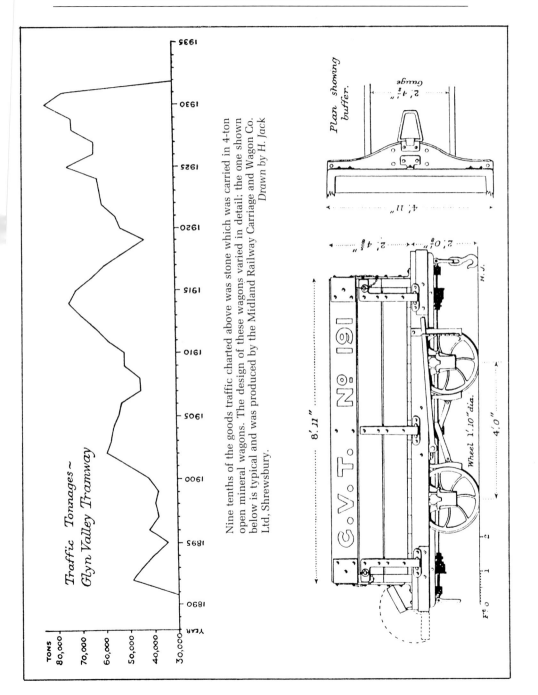

Traffic Tonnages ~
Glyn Valley Tramway

Nine tenths of the goods traffic charted above was stone which was carried in 4-ton open mineral wagons. The design of these wagons varied in detail: the one shown below is typical and was produced by the Midland Railway Carriage and Wagon Co. Ltd, Shrewsbury.

Drawn by H. Jack

Side-tipping wagons at Hendre Quarry. These were only used to take granite from the quarry to the crushers, and did not go out on the main tramway.   *J.I.C. Boyd*

Wagons off the rails, a not uncommon occurrence! On this occasion, in 1904 near Pontfadog church, the cause was recorded as a sheared axle.   *Author's father*

Chapter Four – Pedwar
How the Line was Worked

For the passengers there was a rewarding scenic journey up the valley from Chirk to Glynceiriog, but for the company there was much more than that. At the lower end, a ¾ mile extension ran to the Black Park Lower Wharf. This was one terminus of the early Black Park railway, the other being the Top Wharf, which was on the Holyhead Road and dealt with cart traffic. The old line had been replaced by a branch from the GWR which also served both wharves. The GVT line ran alongside the GWR and then close to the canal before swinging sharply under the GWR to the canal basin. Because of this awkward turn, steam engines did not pass over the final 250 yards of track. At the basin the GVT could take coal direct from the Black Park Colliery, or load and unload into canal barges, the latter traffic of course diminishing as time went on. Henry Dennis also ran here a small pavement slab and street-kerb works, with quarry dust and ballast coming in over the GVT.

In 1906 the canal company, in a last bid for traffic, built a siding, chute and wharf on the canal side proper to save the GVT having to send their wagons to the basin. It was here that road stone was tipped into boats for conveyance to country road sites in Shropshire, a mode of transport that had ceased by the early 1930s. In the opposite direction, narrow boats delivered an occasional load of fine sand which was used by the locomotive for wet rail application. In busier days the shunting work in this area had been done by a horse which lived in a stable beside the chute.

The line then ran south beside the GWR main line track to the two Chirk stations, with workshops and sidings spread over the last third of a mile to the station. These included a carriage shed, stores, smithy, carpenters' shop, engine shed, turntable and an inclined ramp. This last item was the traffic hub of the yard, for over its gravity chutes dropped the bulk of the line's income. The ramp was an earth filled mound about 75 yards long and 12 feet high, faced with masonry on its working side, on to which loaded granite wagons were shunted into two storage sidings at its higher end. To tip their loads, the wagons were allowed to roll back by gravity to one of three tipping positions. There, after brakes had been pinned down, the wheels were clamped to the rails of a rotating device, the side drop door was released and the wagon tilted through 45 degrees by a hand wheel. In this fashion GVT loads were tipped into standard gauge wagons lying alongside at ground level, at the rate of about 200 tons of stone a day. After tipping, wagons ran by gravity into a loop siding to await marshalling into an up train. Other installations included a water column, crane, office, weighing machine, and a slate and goods exchange wharf so sited as to make the floors of the GVT and standard gauge wagons level with one another.

The station at Chirk consisted of a 56 yds-long platform and a building holding booking office and waiting room; it was approached either by road which passed overhead or through a gate from the GWR down platform, which was separated from the GVT platform only by a fence. Just south of this overbridge was a 120 yds-long storage loop for coaches and wagons waiting to be made up into a train.

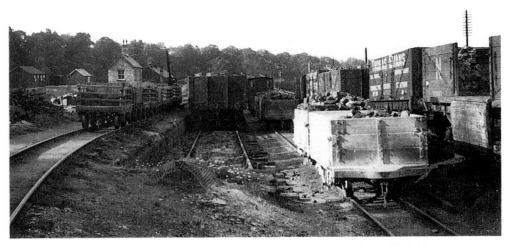

The exchange sidings at Chirk looking to Black Park; the right-hand GVT siding was used for incoming coal.   *Lens of Sutton*

Loading slate on the upper-level siding at the exchange sidings at Chirk.
                                                                                    H.G.W. Household

Locomotive *Dennis* with a mixed train at Pontfadog in May 1932. The waiting room is on the left; however the passing loop is around the corner. *H.C. Casserley*

Sir Theodore on a Chirk train at Pontfadog about 1906. *Lens of Sutton*

After leaving the station, the line ran into a cutting for 500 yards, passing over the canal in its tunnel and then turned westwards, running beside but above the road before entering Baddy's Wood, from which it emerged on the north side of the road. It crossed the road to the south side at Pontfaen 'signal halt'; trains could stop here but seldom did, as there were no houses nearby. A trailing point now led into the 'long siding', a relic of the horse-tram days, 560 yards long, running down to Pontfaen Bridge. There was a name board and a seat on the north side of the road where the line crossed over it.

The line now started its 5½ mile journey beside the road, passing in the first quarter mile Chirk Fish Hatchery. This hatchery, built in 1901, is part of the Chirk Castle Estate and still produces trout fry for the Ceiriog and Dee rivers. At the time of its construction a short siding was put in to supply ballast and dust to make concrete for the 12 fishponds, and it remained there for the rest of the railway's life. Live fish were occasionally shipped down the line in milk churns for export to English waters.

The next stopping place was really a cross between a signal halt and a station, for there were no station buildings and some trains were scheduled to stop whilst others were 'request.' This was Castle Mill and it was at this point that a spur went to the Bronygarth lime-kilns in horse tram days; no siding was put in after 1888. Three-quarters of a mile further on at Herber the former turnpike toll house at the road junction to Bronygarth and Oswestry was reached, which was not a scheduled stopping point. At Herber there was a 50 yds-long siding, 300 yards east of the toll house, where the road widened; the siding lay between the tramway and the road, opposite the old ford from Cae Locyn. Latterly it was used by the Council for delivery of chippings and tar barrels. Prior to 1920 coal was brought here for the use of Bronygarth lime-kilns and lime loaded for up valley destinations.

Four miles from Chirk came the Pontfadog Loop; this lay on a 1 in 130 gradient, up for Glyn trains, and there does not seem to have been a siding. A substantial brick waiting room was provided on the north side of the road, not at the loop but a short distance further towards Glyn.

Pontfadog was followed by the second and last intermediate station at Dolywern, where the road takes an S-bend through the village, To avoid this the line ran on its own property for 250 yards, crossing the Ceiriog river on a single span steel girder bridge supported on dressed stone piers. Immediately beyond, between this bridge and a by-road to the village of Llwyn-mawr, lay the station, which consisted of a private gravel platform at ground level and a brick-built waiting room. On the other side of this platform lay the grounds of the Queen's Head Inn, which in 1909 was converted into a small tourist and fisherman's hotel. On the far side of the road crossing lay an 8-wagon siding and coal yard and then once again the southern side of the main road was regained by the railway. After another mile the outskirts of Glynceiriog were reached where the line again crossed the Ceiriog river on a similar type bridge (Pont Bell) and for a similar reason as at Dolywern.

Just before entering the station, the horse-worked section to the slate quarries diverged, following the road; after a wagon loop, there was the incline running northwards to the Wynne Quarry, followed by the long incline up to the Cambrian Quarry, running west. From the junction, the main line ran gently down into Glyn station, just over 6 miles from Chirk. The old horse-tramway station, reached by a junction a few yards beyond the wagon loop mentioned above, retained a coal platform, water tank, weighing machine, 2-ton crane, and timber yard. However the main coal yard was south of the later station. Passing the engine shed and small turntable on the right beside the main road, the train ran into a loop with the platform on the west side. Beyond this was an ungated level crossing and a long loop with a siding on its east side, after which the line continued to Pandy, with the river below and iron railings above it.

Beyond Glynceiriog the line became a true railway on its own fenced-in right-of-way and after a mile reached Coed-y-Glyn (granite) and Lower Pandy (chinastone) quarries. These quarries were worked between 1885 and 1908 and were provided with extensive sidings, which involved the crossing of the river twice on wooden bridges and the fitting of two track weighing machines. This layout fell into disuse in 1926. A branch to the village of Pandy lay a third of a mile beyond. It consisted of a 1 in 45 curving spur which crossed the valley road by a gated crossing, and ran up into the mouth of the Teirw side valley. Only lightly loaded trains used this spur. For the first eight years of its existence it served the Teirw granite quarry and Pen-y-graig silica quarry, but the former closed in 1896. In later years the top end was dismantled and the spur was used for off-loading coal and goods destined for the higher reaches of the Ceiriog Valley. Between about 1911 and 1920 it also served a silica crushing and extracting plant which was established beside it at its top end.

Meanwhile the mineral main line at Pandy bridged the Ceiriog river for the last time and continued for another three-quarters of a mile to its terminus at the Hendre granite quarry. Here was a layout which allowed wagons on four parallel tracks to be gravity filled with crushed stone. A long dead-end siding on a slight gradient at the far end of the crushing plant allowed empty wagons to run back by gravity under the loading chutes, then onto a weighing machine, and then to be marshalled into a waiting rake of loaded 'down' wagons. A small office and perpetual mantle of white crushing dust completed the scene so far as the GVT was concerned.

The GVT permanent way was made up of 28 ft lengths of flat-bottomed steel rail weighing 50 lb. per yard. These were bolted together with 4-hole 17 in. fish plates and laid on sleepers obtained by cutting down used standard gauge sleepers. When laid in 1888 every 25 foot advance of track cost the company about £2 in materials, with rail accounting for seven-eights of this sum at a price of ½d. lb. Clip and bolt fastenings were used at rail joints, curves and point work, and spikes elsewhere, though this practice was modified in later years in various ways. To maintain the gauge on curves, the rails were cross-tied with spacer rods. The sleepers were spaced about three feet apart and had originally been bedded in gravel ballast 12 inches deep, but as the years went by the ballast became adulterated with other material and eventually the road-bed became a solidified mass.

A good elevated view of Chirk station photographed from the road, in 1931. Note the carriage shed, with a turntable in front.   *R.K. Cope*

This 1932 view of the Chirk engine shed shows that the entrance at the Glyn end was not then in use.   *H.C. Casserley*

Points were close-worked and had their levers counter-balanced. Catch points were fitted at Chirk, Glynceiriog and Hendre to protect main running lines and road crossings. The track was protected by wooden gates or cattle grids whenever it left the main road, and on its own property was always fenced in with 5-bar iron railings. All lineside woodwork was painted white and kept well maintained until the line's closure. The gates at public road crossings opened inwards onto the track and not across the roads, for the railway had no preferential rights-of-way. Such was the route and the track upon which a weekday service was steam operated for nearly half a century.

Traffic on the Glyn Valley Tramway usually consisted of mixed trains or mineral trains, for the only time passenger trains ran unmixed was at Bank Holidays, some summer Saturdays and for organised excursions and outings. For this last kind of traffic often two trains, each of seven coaches, or one consisting of all the coaching stock, would be made up. The demand usually exceeded the fixed supply of 224 seats on these occasions and it was standard practice throughout the life of the line to add dry-stone wagons to the rear of these holiday trains. The wagons would be scrubbed out in the week preceding the event and fitted with wooden forms. Needless to say, such an unusual method of travel had more appeal than conventional carriages and youthful passengers usually made a bee-line for the wagons. Non-operating staff were called in to act as temporary guards to prevent accidents, one person overlooking two or three wagons.

An interesting letter was published in a Shropshire paper from a gentleman who travelled every Friday 80 years ago on the GVT to conduct a bank sub-branch at Glyn. He reported that cyclists often overtook the tram 'and waved in a manner which indicated their superior mode of travel' (the gesture can be imagined). He recalled that one Friday in 1914 the train from Glyn to Chirk was cancelled, and he had to walk to Oswestry and his colleague to Llangollen.

A feature of summer excursion work, which proved very popular, was a round-trip starting at Llangollen. From here a tourist would go by horse-barge down the canal and cross the Pontcysyllte aqueduct to Chirk, where a walk of less than a hundred yards would bring him to the tramway station. Arriving at Glyn, having done 13 miles in splendid ease, he would take to his feet and climb over the hill to Llangollen, an energetic but scenically rewarding 3½ miles. Cheap tickets were issued at Chirk on Monday, Thursdays and Fridays during the summer months and special terms were available for parties of 10 and upwards on other days.

Normal passenger traffic was covered by a minimum service throughout the year, excluding Sundays, of four trains a day in each direction with an extra down train on Wednesdays and Saturdays to meet the demands of market day at Oswestry. Additional trains were introduced in the summer months, which in the summers of 1905–1906 produced a service of nine down and eight up trains a day. This effort placed too great a work load on the engines and in future years only one or, at most, two additional summer trains per day were run. Journey time for the six miles was usually 40 minutes but some down trains were timed for 35 minutes which gave an average speed of 10 mph or 2 mph over the legal maximum. At some time after 1913 the legal limit was increased to 12 mph on enclosed land.

The Working Timetable in the later years shows that one carriage set only was needed for the normal service. The first train, the 6.10 am goods from Chirk, probably had carriages but they are only shown as available for passengers on return from Glyn at 7.40 am. Apart from the first two up trains and the second down one, all were 'mixed'. Three trains per day were shown as running from Hendre Quarries to Glyn in about an hour and a half, from ten to 40 minutes being allowed for shunting at Glyn. Two engines at least would need to be steamed to cope with the passenger service plus the shunting at Hendre and Pandy, and also at Chirk sidings. The table does not show any trains regularly crossing at Pontfadog; trains are shown as 'crossing' at Glyn and Chirk and this presumably refers to engine rosters, as in all cases plenty of time was allowed at the termini for the carriages to lay over.

A set of timetables called the 'Railway Record for Shropshire, North and Mid Wales' showed that, when the steam passenger service commenced, this first train of the day was advertised (Chirk dep. 6.55 am; Glynceiriog arr. 7.45 am) but by 1900, when a GVT timetable appeared in Bradshaw, it was no longer quoted though continued to run as the 'mail'. Mails were carried between 1898 and 1923 and produced an annual revenue of £80. The last up train of the day would wait at Chirk for passengers coming off the London train, which had left Paddington at 2.15 pm, providing notice was given beforehand. By 1907 the maximum waiting period was listed as 15 minutes.

The timetable for the early 1930s presented some odd features: there were five up trains, one headed 'Wednesdays Only' and one 'Not Wednesdays', and six down trains, one headed 'Saturdays Only' and one 'Wednesdays & Saturdays'. This unbalanced appearance was due of course to the fact that the trains were run primarily for the mineral traffic; the train arriving at Glyn Ceiriog at 2.20 normally returned without passengers, but on Saturdays carried the workmen down. Passenger service began at 7.30 am at Glyn Ceiriog and ended at Chirk at 7.44 pm. This connected with the Oswestry railmotor, and 10 minutes later with a train to Ruabon.

Mixed trains always had the coaches marshalled immediately behind the engine (which usually worked running cab-foremost), and a brake van attached to the rear. It was from this van that the guard issued and collected tickets at intermediate stations as there were no staff between Chirk and Glynceiriog. Card tickets were printed for every station and halt in the combination of Singles and Ordinary, Excursion and Market Returns; open Bicycle, Mailcart and Dog tickets were also issued. It was also in the brake van that gunpowder for blasting work in the quarries was conveyed in a locked metal cylinder. The GWR issued three-section tickets at Shrewsbury for the 'tour', Shrewsbury–Chirk (return), Chirk–Glynceiriog, and Llangollen–Chirk. Some tourists did not realise that they needed to walk the missing section.

A mixed train for Glynceiriog might consist of between 10 and 18 vehicles (e.g. 4 coaches, 5 granite wagons, brake van; or 2 coaches, 8 granite wagons, closed van, 6 slate wagons and brake van) and would weigh between 20 and 30 tons, without the locomotive. The mineral wagons would naturally be

A picturesque view of Glynceiriog station about 1895, with the Wynne quarry dominating the village below.   *Courtesy Heyday Publishing*

This early postcard view of the entrance to Chirk station shows the line to the loading ramp (*right*) and a siding at the left of the main line with bolster wagons and a train about to leave the platform.   *Author's Collection*

empty. Down mixed trains were usually of the same size but all the mineral wagons would be loaded, causing the weight of the train to be increased about threefold. Unmixed mineral trains worked from Hendre often consisted of between 15 to 20 loaded granite wagons, which meant that the locomotive and brake van had to be capable of bringing 130 tons to a halt on a falling gradient and wet rail. At the end of each journey the tram engines were turned at Chirk and Glynceiriog.

Hendre Quarry, the largest and only continuously worked stone quarry in the valley, had 2 million tons of its granite removed by the GVT. Though setts and kerb stones were produced in the early days, output became confined to road chippings, tarmacadam, railway ballast and stone dust. Macadam was first produced in 1910 in what had then become the derelict crushing plant of the Lower Pandy Quarry, which was fed with chippings from Hendre Quarry and tar brought from Chirk in a tank mounted in a GVT wagon.

Slate carried by the GVT came from the Wynne and Cambrian Quarries, which were worked intensively as mines between 1890–1909 and 1898–1938 respectively, each producing roughly 2,000 tons of slates per year. In its final form the Cambrian mine had a horizontal main haulage tunnel nearly a mile long, which joined 85 slate extraction chambers at four different levels in the hillside.

The Cambrian mine usually produced six to nine loaded GVT slate trucks a day and these were sent down the half mile gravity incline to Glynceiriog in units of three. The brakesman controlling the drum at the head of the incline would couple up the loaded set to the winding cable, check (with aid of binoculars) that the empties at the bottom showed a white hoist marker and then release the brake of the drum. This caused the empties to be pulled up the 1 in 8 incline by the loaded trucks, with the brakesman checking the speed. This incline was owned and maintained, but not operated by, the GVT Company and was the longest, but not the steepest, of the nine sets of inclines built at varying periods in the area.

The Cambrian and the 150 yds-long Wynne inclines met at their bases, not a hundred yards from the cross-roads at Glynceiriog. Loaded trucks were marshalled at this common base and then run by gravity for 300 yards through the streets to a loop siding, beside the main road and behind the engine shed, to be check-weighed and held for marshalling into a down train. De-railer points prevented a rake running off down the main line should the brakes have failed to hold the loaded wagons on the down grade. Return movements on this, and on the remainder of the track that had been laid at Glynceiriog in the horse-drawn days, were performed by a horse, as the curvature and gradients of the track were unsuitable for the locomotives. The horse was hired from a local farmer to do its daily stint and the annual charge appeared regularly in the 'Traffic Expenses' at the odd figure of £41 14s. 8d.

Two woollen mills at Glynceiriog were also constant but small users of the GVT's goods service. Up to the end of the 1914–18 war nearly half a ton of wool would be carried weekly up valley and return as rolls of flannel, but subsequently mill production declined and became spasmodic.

Operating instructions restricted the loads to be worked on the 1 in 64 gradient between Chirk and Pontfaen signal halt. Up grade the maximum load was restricted to 40 tons behind the engine and down grade to 3 coaches, 32 tons and van, or 50 tons without coaches. Long and heavy trains bound for Chirk were usually divided in two at Pontfaen with the rear half left standing on the track until the engine made a return trip.

The actual wording in the 'General Instructions' was: 'Any train leaving Glyn with more than 60 tons of traffic must be divided at Pontfaen. Before leaving the 'Granite' the Guard in charge of the train must see that a sufficient number of Brakes have been put down, and the Engineman must not start until he has satisfied himself that this has been done'. In the 1920 Instructions the figure was reduced to 50 tons. This is not a very clear instruction, as it is not even certain whether 'traffic' includes tare weight. Also it must be obvious that weather conditions could affect the load that could safely be taken up. It seems likely too that an exact calculation of the weight of a train, if of mixed stock, might be beyond the capacity of some employees. It is known that there were occasions when another train was following and it would be necessary if a train was split, for the rear portion to be lodged in the 'long siding'. There was a short down grade (in the Chirk direction) at the junction, which would have allowed it to be rolled in, but that still leaves a question mark on how it was later drawn out, unless engines were allowed to propel from here to the first Chirk loop.

No signals or train staff control were used, which is highly unusual for a British railway that normally had two engines in steam, but since the GVT was legally a street tramway, the law demanded no distance interval, signals or controls, and none were used. In practice, if trains were to cross en route, instructions were given to the drivers to wait at the only crossing loop at Pontfadog where the points were normally padlocked. That this procedure did not always happen is vividly described by the railway author, L.T.C. Rolt, when he was travelling up the line in about 1930. His Glynceiriog-bound train waited patiently at Pontfadog for a down-valley goods, but as nothing came in sight his train proceeded on its journey only to come to a sharp grinding halt. Just round a corner and partly concealed by a thick hedgerow stood the goods train with a wagon derailed. When this had been rerailed, the goods retreated to Glynceiriog with the passenger train following it.

In its journey up the valley the tramway rose about 220 feet and the gradients were easy except for two short stretches: from Pontfaen eastwards half a mile of 1 in 40/50 up, and another half mile of 1 in 45/65 up to the Glyn terminus. There were some sharp gradients on the Hendre extension, but they were 'with the load'.

Accidents on the line were fortunately few and were usually derailments caused by track or axle failure. An accident causing bodily injury occurred in 1899 or 1900 which involved the GVT in compensation payments of: £280 – passengers or wayfarers, £30 – employee, £7 – goods. No details of this incident now survive. In 1918 an evening train was heading up the Pontfaen–Chirk gradient in wild and dark weather when it gave a glancing blow to a tree, that had been brought down by the storm. The locomotive

One of the two brake vans on a mixed train standing at Glynceiriog platform about 1920, seen from the Hendre end. *Lens of Sutton*

Another early view of Glynceiriog station, taken from the level crossing at the Hendre end. *Lens of Sutton*

carried an acetylene lamp but its rays did not pitch very far and it was nearly upon the obstruction with full regulator before the crew saw it. The cab of the tram engine, which as usual was travelling first, was badly damaged but fortunately no one was injured. A major accident occurred in January 1919 on the same gradient when a 46-year old guard was seriously injured by a piece of timber when attempting to secure a load that had worked loose on a bolster wagon. The employee died of his injuries. In 1928 a down mineral train hit a car parked across the track and hidden by a curve at Pontfadog church. The owners escaped injury as they were visiting a grave in the churchyard but the car was damaged as it was flung off the track. In June 1932 a 60-year-old driver died as the indirect result of a near collision between his locomotive and a lorry at Hendre Quarry. For the public the safety record, covering 50 years, is a good one when considering that the line crossed six ungated public roads, innumerable field and lane crossings, lay beside the main road for five miles, and worked across the crossroads at Glynceiriog.

The staff needed to work this line throughout its life numbered about thirty. The normal complement was:

1 General Manager and Secretary	1 shunter/brakesman (Glyn)
1 station master/clerk (Chirk)	5 permanent way workers
1 station master/clerk (Glyn)	2 blacksmith/fitters
1 locomotive foreman/driver	5 joiners
3 drivers	2 locomotive/carriage cleaners
4 firemen	4 yard loaders (Chirk)
2 guards	

Total: 32 employees.

The Chirk depot staff of nine men was certainly not excessive when it is realised that two engines had continually to be kept in steam and that, in addition to running repairs, all locomotives and an annual average of 7 coaches and 155 wagons were given overhauls. All staff worked a day shift except the two locomotive cleaners, who worked through the night preparing the two (usually) engines for the next day's run. After a general clean, the fires were lit in the early morning and with a head of 40 lb. pressure of steam the cleaners could gently move their charges to the coaling point. The train crews worked a double day shift to cover the period 6 am–9 pm, with the rest of the staff working a normal day. The permanent way staff had no sinecure either for, in addition to normal plate-laying work, they had to keep the road hedges trimmed in the summer. The clearance between coaches and the hedge was so small that passengers in open coaches would get a switch across the face unless the new shoots were continually cut back. Several employees of the line belonged to the National Union of Railwaymen; there were no trade disputes except for the General Strike of 1926 when all GVT employees withdrew their labour in common with all other railway workers. In character with the line, the staff wore no uniform.

Sir Theodore on a mineral train, taking the gradient to the east of Pontfaen about 1930.
Ken Nunn Collection

Chapter Five – Pump
From Moderate Success to Closure

Although the GVT was built as a slate tramway, it is important to realise that for most of its life its principal traffic was granite. From 1888 onwards stone comprised 89 per cent of the tonnages and 68 per cent of all traffic revenues. In the 46 full years of steam operation between 1889 and 1934 the trend of the tonnages carried annually rose slowly; though this was masked by considerable annual fluctuations. The average annual tonnage was 52,000 tons. In the first half of the 46-year-period there were only five years (1902–1906) in which the average annual tonnage was exceeded, whilst in the second half there were only six years (1918–21 and 1932–34) in which it was not. It is ironic that the highest annual tonnage ever carried by the GVT was achieved in 1930 with 82,958 tons, when defeat by world-wide economic stagnation and road vehicles lay round the corner.

The total freight tonnages (with their revenue percentages given in brackets) for the 46 years consisted of: Stone – 89% (80% £); Coal, coke, lime, etc. – 4½% (6½% £); Slate – 4% (2½% £); Merchandise – 2½% (11% £). In the second half of the period under review these statistics would be equivalent of the following number of loaded wagons worked in one day: Down trains – 47 granite wagons and 9 slate trucks; Up trains – 3 mineral four-ton wagons, and 2 vans or 3 two-ton open wagons.

Passenger traffic for the 42 years, 1891–1932 inclusive, was almost exclusively 3rd class, for only 1 per cent of all passengers paid 1st class fares, which incidentally provided 2 per cent of the passenger revenue. The passenger traffic showed the same upward trend as the freight but its peaks and troughs were less pronounced. There was a steady annual rise to 1906 when 37,172 passengers were carried. Between 1907 and 1929 the annual traffic varied between the limits of 33,500 and 42,500 passengers, with two exceptional years of 1919 and 1920 when 53,720 and 49,084 passengers were carried. It is probable that tourists provided two-thirds of this traffic between the months of May and September. Passengers and mails, which were always considered a by-product of mineral traffic, contributed 16½ per cent of the traffic receipts for the period 1891–1932.

Passenger fares and goods charges showed considerable stability though the inflationary trends of World War I caused the company to make a minor increase in 1917 and a further one in 1919. The list shows the charges for 1900 which for passenger fares had altered little by 1933.

Third Class Single Fares:		*Goods per ton per mile:*	
Chirk to:		Stone, Coal	2d.
Pontfaen	1½d.	Slate	3½d.
Castle Mill	3d.	Grain	7¾d.
Pontfadog	5d.	Produce	5d.–8d.
Dolywern	7d.	Hay	10¾d.
Glynceiriog	8d.	General goods	9½d.–1s. 1d.

Return fares were issued, which in the case of a Chirk to Glynceiriog ticket showed a saving of 2d. over the single fares. First class fares were double the thirds. Excursion tickets were issued which gave small monetary concessions and during and just after the 1914–18 war there were some 30 season ticket holders.

The pre-1917 charge for transporting a loaded 4 ton wagon from Hendre quarry to the GWR at Chirk was 5s. 4d., whilst a 1 ton truck of slate from the Cambrian quarry to Chirk was charged 1s. 10¾d. (or 7s. 7d. for 4 tons). These charges naturally included the cost to the GVT of hauling the empty wagons back up the valley, and terminal and transhipment expenses. It is interesting to see that the company would not carry, except on special conditions, 'gunpowder, lucifer matches, aquafortis, oil of vitriol, and other dangerous articles.'

The expenses in running the line before World War I were on average 68 per cent of traffic receipts and after it 88 per cent. About three-fifths of these expenses consisted of materials, services and taxes, and the remaining two-fifths covered labour costs. Looked at in another way the expenses consisted of:

Locomotive running	33%	Track maintenance	12%
Repair of locomotives/vehicles	19%	General charges	11%
Traffic working	18%	Rates and taxes	7%

Annual net income varied considerably but the average for the 46 years under review was just over £1,000. The inflationary period of and after World War I meant however that income was falling relative to the capital employed. For instance the net annual incomes of £1,181 in 1903 and £1,143 in 1927 are not comparable.

The golden era of the tramway was the 20-odd years up to World War I. A decline set in during this war, caused by the considerable reduction in the amount of minerals carried and the rapid rise of labour and material costs. This trend, plus a locomotive purchase and repair bill of £3,322 in 1921, caused no profits to be made between 1919 and 1926. After 1921 a gross profit was made, which was used to pay off the outstanding debit balance which included a loan of £2,000 from Beyer Peacock Ltd, for an additional and second-hand locomotive, repayable at the rate of £400 per annum. In 1932 the company again made an annual loss and continued to do so until closure in 1935. The post-1920 financial performance was most creditable considering all the adverse factors working against the GVT.

Out of the average annual income of £1,000, interest payments on loan capital absorbed about £600, leaving £400 to be paid to shareholders or put to reserve. This meant that shareholders received over the years a 1 per cent dividend for their investment.

The authorised capital of this private company was £73,000 and the paid-up amount had stabilised at about £63,000 by 1895. There was £24,295 in Ordinary shares, £26,377 in 5 per cent Cumulative Preference shares and Loans of about £13,000. The loan capital fluctuated between £8,500 and £18,250 and had varying interest rates of 4½, 5 and 6 per cent. This loan capital always received preferential treatment when the annual income was being disbursed, with the result that the 5 per cent Preference shareholders only received a 5 per cent dividend in 1892 and 1893 and nothing at all after 1916. At the end of 1934 the dividend arrears for this class of shareholder amounted to the meaningless sum, by then, of £50,495. To make neither profit nor loss the line required a minimum granite traffic of about 45/50,000 tons per year and a small amount of miscellaneous traffic. Red figures would appear in the finances if the volume of granite traffic dropped appreciably, or the wages bill rose considerably, or a large expense such as the purchase of a locomotive was incurred. Without passengers a small credit balance could still be maintained, but loss of granite traffic spelt debt and doom and this is what happened when in 1932 the line carried only 21,400 tons of granite, as compared with 69,900 tons in the previous year.

Because 1913 is a typical year in the life of the GVT and is about mid-point in the steam passenger-carrying era, it has been selected to show a set of annual accounts in detail:

Income: 1913

		£	
Granite	62,226 tons	2,845	(59% of traffic receipts)
Merchandise	908 tons	368	(8% of traffic receipts)
Coal, Coke	3,234 tons	340	(7% of traffic receipts)
Slate	3,100 tons	272	(6% of traffic receipts)
Passengers	40,600 3rds	877 ⎱	(18% of traffic receipts)
	394 1sts	18 ⎰	
Mail: G.P.O. Contract		80	(2% of traffic receipts)
Land rent and interest		66	
	Income	£4,866	

Expenditure: 1913

		£	
Locomotive running expenses		1,037	(22% of traffic receipts)
Repair of: locomotives	£118		
coaches	£151		
wagons	£371	640	(13% of traffic receipts)
Traffic running expenses		594	(12% of traffic receipts)
Maintenance of way and works		390	(8% of traffic receipts)
General administrative charges		393	(8% of traffic receipts)
Rates and Taxes		240	(5% of traffic receipts)
	Expenditure £3,296		(68% of traffic receipts)

Excess of income over expenditure: £1,570.
Deduction of £757 for rent charges (£108) and loans interest (£649).
Balance of £813 to be carried to Debentures Redemption Account.

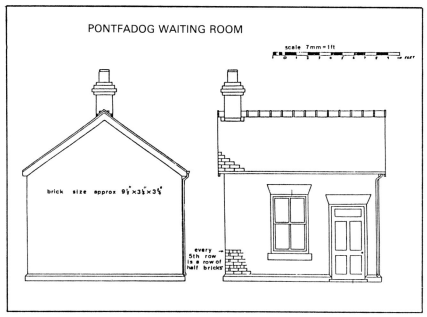

Courtesy of Glyn Valley Tramway Group

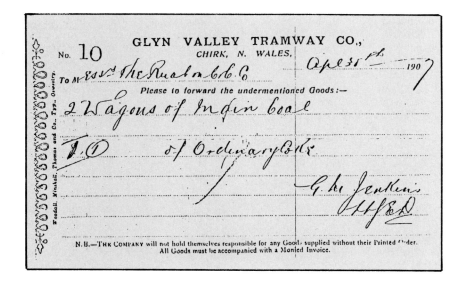

The locomotive running expenses, which were the largest single item of expenditure, consisted of: Wages £534, Coal £411, Lubricants £73, and Water £19. Wages accounted for four-fifths of the traffic running expenses of £594, whilst the administrative charges included Directors' fees of £60, auditors' charge of £10 and the General Manager's salary of £250.

Loaded train mileage during the last 20 years of the tramway was fairly constant at 32,000–35,000 miles per annum. As the Working Timetable required only 530 miles per week to be worked (27,500 per annum) it seems that excursions and extra mineral trips to the number of about 10 per week must have been run).

For most of its steam days the Glyn Valley Tramway performed its daily task without fuss or flourish and only occasionally was the routine broken by some event or drama. Sometimes it was the river Ceiriog which caused the break, for though placid in the summer it could rise rapidly in winter-time, causing the railway to be threatened by its foaming waters at about eight different spots.

On the last day of 1900 the river washed out the road completely and undermined the rail track (which was on the far side of the road to the river) so as to leave it dangling in mid air at a point a half-mile south of Glyn-ceiriog. An oil painting of the scene hangs in the Ceiriog Memorial Institute at that village. It took a week's work to resume normal services and cost Denbighshire County Council £2,000 to make good the damage. A retaining wall was later built along this section to protect road and tramway from the occasional turbulences of the Ceiriog River.

Just as two engines of the Snailbeach Railway helped to work the GVT for a short period in 1887–1888, so a return visit was paid by a GVT locomotive in 1905. In that year the Ceiriog Granite Co. opened a quarry close to the Snailbeach Railway and a branch line of that railway was laid to serve it. The Snailbeach Railway lacked dependable engines and Henry Dennis, who served on the Boards of both companies, arranged that Sir Theodore be sent to Snailbeach on loan to help work the branch until new motive power was obtained. Unfortunately the loan was not a success because the gauges of the Glyn Valley Tramway and Snailbeach Railway varied by half an inch, the former 2 ft 4½ in. and the latter 2 ft 4 in. The wheel flanges of Sir Theodore kept riding up and on to the top of the rails causing frequent derailment, and so, in disgrace, she was returned to her home line.

Henry Dennis, the persistent force behind the gestation and birth of the GVT, died in 1906 at the age of 81. In the later part of his life he held large and varied financial interests in collieries, clay works, water and gas under-takings and limestone quarries, and it is estimated that at the zenith of his career the various concerns under his indirect control employed nearly 10,000 persons. When Sir Theodore Martin, Chairman of the company, died in 1909, it was a son of Henry Dennis, Dyke Dennis, who succeeded him and remained as Chairman until the GVT ceased to exist. In this way the Dennis family was closely associated with the GVT from its conception to its dying days.

World War I caused a decline in quarry labour forces to the point where only 20 men worked on slate production in the valley. This contraction could not be tolerated in the Hendre granite quarry as large quantities of crushed stone were needed for road and concrete work, and so in due course 150 German prisoners-of-war were put to work in it. They arrived in a GVT train and were housed in a camp built near the crushing plant. As prisoners-of-war they remained loyal to their country, for in 1914 one hundred and nine free men produced 66,500 tons of stone whilst in 1918 one hundred and sixty-four men, mostly in bondage, won only 45,200 tons.

In 1923 Warrington Corporation sought without success to build two dams in the upper part of the valley above Hendre Quarry. This would have brought additional revenue and track mileage to the GVT but would have drowned 45 farms, 37 houses and 19 other buildings such as schools, chapels and shops.

In the same year another link with early GVT days was broken when G.M. Jenkins, the General Manager and Secretary, died in harness after 32 years in that post. He was the man responsible for the day to day operation of the tramway and had watched and nursed it to maturity. Albert Wynn, his successor, who held the post until the tramway's demise, immediately instituted an extensive re-sleepering and wagon repair programme, for the number of derailments and derelict wagons was becoming burdensome.

Originally the flat bottomed rails had been laid directly on top of the wooden sleepers, but the latter were now rotting and so allowed the rail to sink into the wood. The passage of trains caused the rails to splay out at an angle which opened the gauge and derailed vehicles; in some cases wagons holding tarmac had careered into the river Ceiriog, causing pollution problems, and on one occasion *Sir Theodore* dropped between the rails. Sleepers were normally replaced at the rate of about 400 a year but between 1924 and 1931 three-quarters of the 'main' line was renewed, with a peak figure of 2,220 sleepers in 1928. To avoid a repetition of the cause of derailments, a ten inch square metal plate was placed between the rail and sleeper to spread the load. Between 1925 and 1932 fifty wagons were given a heavy repair annually, which was something that had not been attempted before. This involved extensive repairs to the frame and the replacement of broken axles and worn fittings.

The cartage monopoly of the GVT at Hendre Quarry was broken in 1926 when a motor access road was built between the valley main road and the quarry. Tarmac production was transferred from Lower Pandy to Hendre Quarry and thereafter lorries took the tarmac away by road to allow it to be worked 'hot' on site. It was not long before lorries were carting chippings direct to road resurfacing works.

The year 1932 was one that tolled the bell for the GVT and foretold the line's closure three years later. At this time there was mass unemployment and the country's economy was in a parlous state. No expenditure on a national or county basis was made unless the need was imperative and this naturally reduced road construction and maintenance. The 1932 Annual Report of the company was sombre and accurate when it said: 'The national economy campaign has had disastrous effects on the road stone quarrying industry upon which the tramway depends principally for its revenue.

Every effort has been made during the year to reduce the expenditure to the minimum and if trade does not improve, there is no alternative but to close down.'

In the same year, a motor bus service was inaugurated in the valley which gave a more direct route to the market town of Oswestry. So far as passenger traffic was concerned the result was a foregone conclusion and on Thursday 6th April, 1933, all passenger trains ceased to run.

As for mineral traffic, the GVT struck back against its competitors and arranged in 1934 for road lorries to be loaded at Chirk at the railway gravity chutes, thus retaining 4,000 tons of traffic which otherwise would have gone direct by road from Hendre. But the GVT was waging a losing battle, for the lorry was a more flexible and less costly form of transport involving no transhipment work. In a way it is sad to think the GVT took a hand in its own death, in the sense that all the road stone it carried contributed to the making of roads suitable for motorised traffic which eventually supplanted it.

Losses of £420, £212 and £321 had been made in working the line in 1932, 1933 and 1934. The Directors knew this could never be made good, so it was decided the line should be closed to all traffic after 62 years of service, of which period 47 years were in steam. Although the official closing date as recorded by the Railway Clearing House was Saturday 6th July, 1934, it appears from a report in the *Border Counties Advertizer* of 3rd July that the last revenue-producing train had run on 29th June, a week earlier. It stated 'The Glyn Valley Tramway ceased to function on Saturday . . . when it was learned last week that Saturday would be the last day for the train to run, scores of people at Glyn Ceiriog and all along the route to Chirk waited to see the train coming down for the last time'. No doubt the clearing-up operations meant that occasional workings occurred up to and perhaps beyond Saturday 6th July, but the tramway's history really came to an end on 29th June.

The table below, which gives all figures in thousands, shows the rapid decline in traffic in the last three complete years of operation. The figures for 1929 are typical of the preceding twenty years:

Decline of GVT Traffic (figures in thousands)

Year	No. of passengers	Granite	Freight in Tons Slate	Coal	General	Locomotive Miles Train	Shunt
1929	33.7	64.8	3.8	2.2	1.7	36.6	7.4
1930	27.8	75.9	3.2	1.9	1.8	37.6	7.6
1931	24.1	69.9	2.7	1.7	1.3	36.4	7.3
1932	13.1	21.4	2.2	1.3	0.5	16.4	3.1
1933	0.5	20.1	3.0	1.2	0.4	8.1	3.3
1934	Nil	25.8	2.9	0.8	0.4	8.2	4.4

In September 1935 the GVT was converted into a limited company and at an extraordinary general meeting held in October it was decided to wind-up the business and put the company into voluntary liquidation. In the following year a Wrexham firm lifted the rails by lorry, the locomotives were cut up for scrap at Chirk, the carriages (less frames and wheels) were sold for outhouses, and the metal of the wagons went for scrap. A considerable number of GVT rails were sold to Gresford Colliery and laid in one of the main underground roadways. This Wrexham pit had suffered a disaster in 1935, involving the loss of 264 lives and an abandonment of much of the underground workings, and it was in the new workings that the rails were used. The final episode of the GVT's history took place on 7th January, 1938, when the liquidator presented his winding-up report to a meeting of creditors and shareholders at Chester.

Miraculously, two Glyn Valley carriages survived to run again. These were the first class coach (believed to have been No. 14) and a similar third-class one. The former had three owners as a shed before its body was bought from Chirk vicarage by the Talyllyn Railway, refurbished and placed on new running gear. It entered TR service in 1958 as 1st class No. 14. Shortly after, the third class body was purchased; this had had two owners and came from a farm near Glynceiriog. It was in poor condition but was rebuilt by Hunt Bros of Oldbury, and went into service on the TR as first-class coach No. 15. Both were re-painted in GVT livery, with garter monograms; roof lamps had to be removed owing to the lower bridge heights.

The two covered vans were purchased for use as sheds at Vron Quarry, Llangollen, where they lasted some 35 years more as grounded bodies. The fate of the guards' vans has not been recorded.

Some of the rails were sent over to the Canal Foundry at Trevor for passing on to Sheffield scrap merchants. Some were sold to the Talyllyn Railway and are still (1990) in use; others went, as already mentioned, to the Union Colliery at Gresford.

An interesting 1932 view of *Dennis*, with its skirting plates lifted.   *H.C. Casserley*

At Chirk itself, some industrial activity continued after the closure of the tramway. Though the metal mines had long gone, the Black Park Colliery remained working until 1952; some 350 years of mining, though not in exactly the same location over the years. The last coal mine in the area was at Ifton, St Martins, closed in 1968. The canal, now called the Llangollen Canal under British Waterways, maintained some vestigial commercial carrying until 1940. Recently it has enjoyed a boom in leisure traffic by private and hired narrow boats. The Pontstycyllte viaduct, the crossing of which can be a vertiginous experience, has an enormous fascination for tourists. Local pictorial guides include interesting photographs, mostly old postcards, featuring the Tramway, and 55 years after it closed enthusiasts still search eagerly for any remaining signs of its existence. It will certainly not be forgotten.

Postscript – What Remains Today

The remains of the tramway were long-lasting and in some cases still exist today (1990).

Chirk: all remaining GVT buildings in the yard were demolished in 1969 and the area is now an industrial estate. In the station, the platform remains although the trackbed is filled in almost to platform height. The station building went in 1968, and the steps from the road to the GVT platform in 1977. Hand Lane bridge is still there.

Chirk to Pontfaen: Lever's footbridge over the formation is extant, the timber superstructure having been renewed in 1977 to the original design. The formation through the Castle estate and Baddy's Wood is very overgrown.

Pontfaen: the formation is still traceable coming down the gradient to the road (most trackbed by the roadside was obliterated in 1936 by a new water main and road widening).

Herber Siding: is still recognisable as a wide verge.

Pontfadog: the site of the loop is recognisable by the wide verge used by Clwyd C.C. The waiting room was purchased in 1989 by the GVT Society and is being renovated.

Dolywern: the deviation formation is still *in situ* and culvert and river bridge extant. The trackbed was severed by an extension to the Cheshire Home. The station building is there but semi-derelict. The coal yard exists, still fenced by GVT iron bar fencing.

Glynceiriog: the engine shed is extant and used by Clwyd C.C., smoke cowls removed, and re-roofed, doors steel-cladded. The station building is still there but much altered and a private dwelling; the platform remains.

The trackbed of the Dolywern deviation after track lifting; the bridge over the river is just right of the pine tree. *Author's Collection*

The GVT tramway side of Chirk station after demolition. *Photomatic Ltd*

The coal office is extant, with chimney removed and re-roofed 1984. New window frames and glazing supplied by GVT Society were fitted in 1985. Most of the buildings and iron fencing in the coal yard are still there. The horse tramway sections in the village have been obliterated but the two inclines can still be noted on the hillside.

Glyn to Pont-y-Meibon: a large section of the trackbed at Ddol-hir, (between Glynceiriog and Coed-y-Glyn) was obliterated in 1982. Between there and Pont-y-Meibon was given to the National Trust in 1948 and later, opened up as the 'Glyn Valley Tramway Walk'. The bridge abutments to the line to lower Pandy chinastone quarry are extant in the river bed at Coed-y-Glyn, Pandy river bridge is *in situ,* and the formation onwards to Upper Pandy granite quarry traceable. All trackbed beyond Pont-y-Meibon into Hendre is now private but some quarry buildings remain as ruins.

A section of the line between Hendre and Pandy used only by granite traffic (c.1900) looking down the valley. *Locomotive Publishing Co.*

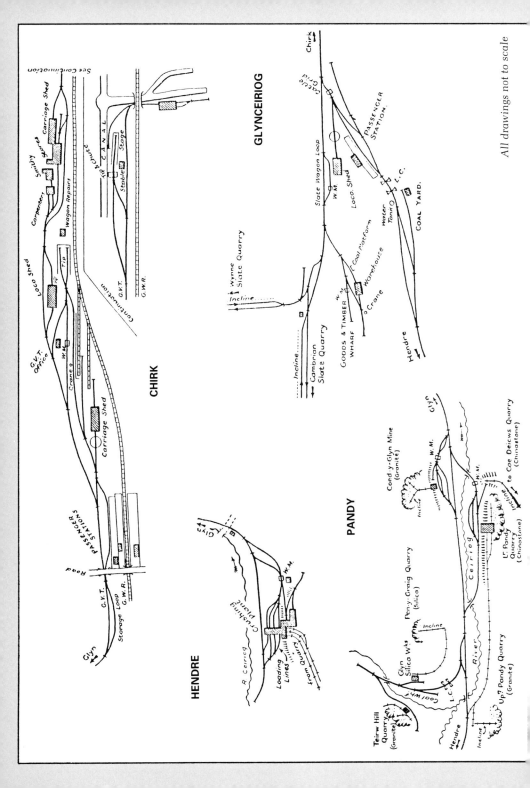

All drawings not to scale

CHIRK

See Continuation

Carriage Shed
Sawer
Smithy
Carpentry
Wagon Repairs
Tip Chute
Stage
Stable
G.W.R.
O.V.T.
Continuation
CANAL
Tip
Loco Shed
G.V.T. Office
W.M.
Crane
Carriage Shed
PASSENGERS
Road
G.V.T.
Storage Loop G.W.R.
Glyn

GLYNCEIRIOG

Chirk
Cattle Grid
Slate Wagon Loop
W.M.
Loco Shed
PASSENGER STATION.
L.C.
Water Tank
COAL YARD.
Warehouse
Crane
Coal Platform
W.M.
GOODS & TIMBER WHARF
Incline
Cambrian Slate Quarry
Wynne Slate Quarry
Incline
Hendre

HENDRE

Exit
Tip
W.M.
Crushing Plant
R. Ceiriog
Loading Lines
from Quarry

PANDY

Coed-y-Glyn Mine (Granite)
Incline
W.M.
Glyn
to Coe Deicws Quarry (Chinastone)
Lr Pandy Quarry (Chinastone)
W.M.
Ceiriog
Pen-y-Graig Quarry (Silica)
Incline
Glyn Silica Wks
Coal Wharf
L.C.
River Ceiriog
Hendre
Incline
Up.r Pandy Quarry (Granite)
Teirw Hill Quarry (Granite)

Appendix One
Route Details

Location	Distance Chirk Station M. F.	Height above: Sea Level Feet	Pontfaen Feet	Details
CANAL BASIN AND WHARF	0 6	310	23	Coal exchange siding at Black Park Basin with Colliery. Canal side stone loading tip.
GVT Yards	0 3 to 0 0	330	43	Carriage shed, stores, smithy, carpenters' shop, granite tip wharf (to GWR), locomotive (and repair) shed, office, track weighing machine, crane, transhipment wharf (GVT–GWR), turntable, sidings.
CHIRK STATION	0 0	340	53	Raised platform, booking office, waiting room, water point, running loops.
Chirk–Pontfaen Bank	–	–	–	¾ mile long. Gradient 1 in 64.
*PONTFAEN HALT	0 7½	287	0	Line gained and crossed valley main road. Long siding ran back down valley to Pontfaen bridge for 560 yards.
*Fish Hatchery	1 2	297	10	One 15 yard siding on private property.
*CASTLE MILL HALT	1 6	326	39	Nameboard only.
*Herber Sidings	2 4½	362	75	One 65 yard siding.
*PONTFADOG STATION	3 6	420	133	150 yard crossing loop, waiting room.
Bridge No. 1	4 6	475	188	Crossed river Ceiriog. One steel arch of 25 ft span, 13 ft high. Dressed stone abutments.
DOLYWERN STATION	4 6½	475	188	Private but unraised platform, waiting room, private goods yard with one 35 yard siding and weighing machine.
Bridge No. 2	5 7	533	246	Crossed river Ceiriog. Details as for No. 1.
GLYNCEIRIOG	6 1½	550 to 570	263 to 283	Station: Raised platform, station offices, locomotive shed, turntable, running loop, siding. Coal Yard: 1,200 gall. water tank, running loop, coal siding, weighing machine. *Village: 300 yard spur leading to former terminus of horse tramway and to the two inclines. Slate loop with track weighing machine, goods shed, timber wharf, 2-ton crane, 10 ton track weighing machine.

Coed-y-Glyn and Lower Pandy Quarries	7	0	620	333	Loop sidings and running loops totalling 1,100 yds, two wooden river bridges, two track weighing machines. Disused after 1926.
Pandy Spur Junction	7	3	655	368	Loop. 350 yds spur crossing main road to Pandy village with one 70 yds siding and weighing machine.
Bridge No. 3	7	3½	660	373	Crossed river Ceiriog. Details as for No. 1.
HENDRE QUARRY:					
Entrance	7	7½	703	416	Four loop sidings with stone gravity loaders overhead, running loops, track weighing machines, office.
Dead End	8	1½	715	428	

Track Mileage

Passenger: Chirk to Glynceiriog	6 miles 1½ furlongs
Goods: Canal to Hendre Quarry	8 miles 7 furlongs
(Officially recorded as 8 m. 63 chains)	
Sidings, loops, spurs and incline	About 5 miles 1 furlong
Total track length	14 miles (Approx.)

SLATE MINE INCLINES – **Cambrian:** 925 yds long at 1 in 8 rising 370 ft to 940 ft a.s.l.
Wynne: 150 yds long at 1 in 3 rising 130 ft to 700 ft above sea level.

* = Points at which line was at roadside.

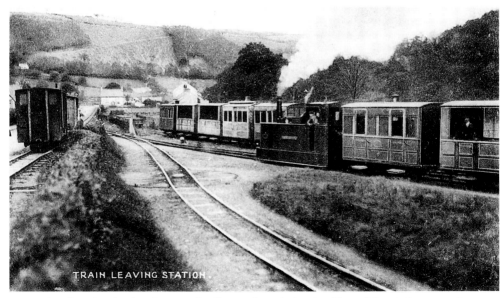

TRAIN LEAVING STATION.

Another view by the photographer Burns of a train leaving Glynceiriog station around 1923; the mineral train on the left is standing on the connection to the quarries; note the turntable on the left of the engine.   *Author's Collection*

Appendix Two
1920 Committee Report

The Ministry of Transport set up a Light Railways (Investigation) Committee in 1920. It was appointed to examine the possible future development of Light Railways in the UK, and sent detailed questionnaires to all light railways; that sent to G.M. Jenkins, Secretary and Manager of the GVT, was received on 17th July, 1920 and returned on 29th October. His replies were lucid and comprehensive and are useful as a guide to the working of the tramway in the period 1910–20. The following are points of interest culled from the 36 foolscap sheets of the returned questionnaire:

10 & 11: livestock in the valley is disposed of at Glyn, Llangollen and Oswestry and generally carried by road. No provision is made to carry livestock on the GVT.

13: there is practically no road competition. A little coal is carried between Chirk and Pontfadog by farmers who occupy small-holdings. All coal for places beyond is carried by train.

14: permanent way: the ballast is gravel, one foot below sleepers (size 5 ft × 10 in. × 5 in.). Rails are f.b. steel 50 lb. per yard in 28 ft lengths. The maximum gradient is 1 in 25 and ruling gradient 1 in 50. Minimum radius of curves on main line is 3 chains (200 ft) and in sidings 6 chains.

15: maximum axle loads: used 2 tons, permitted 2½ tons.

16: maximum speed of trains: (a) inclusive 'booked', 10 mph along road, 12 mph on enclosed land; (b) authorised, the same; (c) safely possible, 20 mph.

17: mileage fenced along track 3¼ miles.

19: the cost of the three bridges over the Ceiriog was about £200 each.

21: the height loading gauge is governed by the Chirk road overbridge which is 13 ft 6 in. from rail level.

24: traffic at halts: dealt with by guards issuing tickets from van. Very few parcels are dealt with. At Pontfaen no parcels or merchandise are dealt with; at Castle Mill parcels are left at a cottage a few feet away. There are mineral sidings at Pontfaen, Herber and Pandy. The number of intermediate sidings total five, two controlled from Chirk and the remainder from Glyn; principally used for coal and mineral traffic.

26: station accommodation: Chirk, waiting room and booking office. Glyn, waiting rooms, booking office, goods merchandise and engine shed. Pontfadog and Dolywern, waiting room at each halt. Chirk platform is 56 yards long, average width 13 ft, 2 ft 3 in. high. Cranes at Chirk and Glyn are 2 tons capacity. Weighbridges at Chirk and Glyn have 10 tons capacity. All transhipment at Chirk is done by hand, except stone tipping, at a cost of about 1s. per ton in 1920. Very little traffic is received by canal and is dealt with by hand. Stone for canal dispatch is unloaded by an elevated tipper.

27: workshops: no heavy repairs are undertaken. For locomotives these are carried out by Beyer Peacock & Co. All light repairs to wagons and coaches are dealt with, but repairs to wheels and axles are done by Messrs Hadfields of Sheffield.

28: rolling stock: the whole of the stock is owned by the GVT Co., except 20 wagons belonging to the Ceiriog Granite Co.

31: the number of engines in use (steam) daily is 2.

32: brakes: coaches, chain brake applied by hand. Freight, hand brake fitted to each wagon.

33 & 34: [answers here are rather odd: three locomotives are used but when weights of these are requested, only details of the Baldwin, not yet purchased, are given: states total weight 14 tons 11 cwt., with 10½ × 16 cylinders, 140 lb. boiler pressure.]

38: water supply, two points only, Chirk direct from main; Glyn, stored in 1,200 gallon tank, no pumping involved.

41: number of vehicles in train (quotes mixed trains only): coaches and empty stock, max. 20 vehicles, average 18. Coaches and full trucks, max. 12 vehicles up valley and 20 down, average 12.

42: maximum gross load handled by locomotive; up, 30 tons, down 130 tons.

43: type of buffers and drawgear: solid buffers on rolling stock except passenger coaches which have spring buffers. Spring drawboards on passenger coaches and one half on trucks. Quite satisfactory.

44: coach lighting: colza oil but steps are being taken to light with acetylene gas. No coach heating.

47: train running: worked by two [one inserted by clerk and altered by Jenkins] engines in steam. Fixed crossing places are arranged by notice. No train staff or ticket used. Trains do not stop between halts to pick up or set down passengers.

57: the line is administered by a Board of Directors and Secretary and Manager, and is worked by a staff of 28 men. No part-timers. Train staff, 11 men. Station staff, 7 men. Maintenance staff, 10 men.

69: the total cost of constructing the line, less rolling stock, maintenance and repair works and plant, was £63,628. Part of the line runs over land for which rental is paid. The total cost of rolling stock was £9,112 and repair plant etc. was £500.

In general comments, Jenkins makes the point that narrow-gauge lines must make charges equal or less than standard gauge lines and that these charges must include transhipment expenses. If not, the customer will take his own transport to the nearest standard gauge station. He suggests that the speed limit be increased to 15–20 mph to make working more economical.

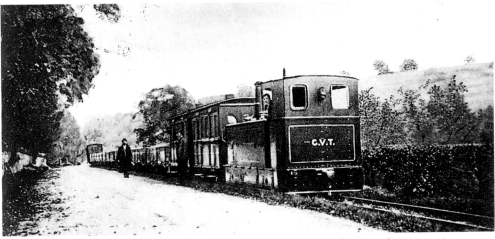

A postcard view of a train at Pontfaen around 1906 showing the interesting locomotive-end livery.   *Author's Collection*

A mixed train at Chirk station platform in May 1932.   *H.C. Casserley*

A train of roadstone from Hendre apparently having problems prior to entering Glynceiriog station about 1920.   *National Railway Museum*

Appendix Three
Traffic

These statistics relate to the steam traction period. The annual average is obtained by dividing the totals by 46 (1889–1934 inclusive) except in the case of passenger traffic where the divisor is 42 (1891–1932 inclusive). The monetary items are not strictly comparable as the value of the £ fell considerably in 1914–18 period.

Item	Three Typical Years			Annual Average
	1897	1911	1925	
Locomotive miles	33,227	45,195	47,898	36,300
1st class passengers	293	496	247	344
3rd class passengers	24,848	39,741	42,006	33,065
Merchandise, tons	994	910	2,531	1,295
Minerals, tons	37,292	57,028	72,040	50,753
Passenger/mail revenue	£ 591	£ 987	£1,212	£ 929
Merchandise	£ 311	£ 374	£ 852	£ 465
Mineral	£2,376	£3,085	£7,843	£3,814
Receipts, all sources	£3,382	£4,498	£9,966	£5,169
Working expenditure	£2,173	£2,897	£7,879	£4,133
Net income	£1,209	£1,601	£2,087	£1,036

Totals for all years:

Passengers: 1,403,224   Net income: £47,648
Freight (tons): 2,394,234   Locomotive miles: 1,663,800

Quarries served by GVT

These are arranged in rough order of importance, *Persons employed* is given as an indication of size but it must be stressed that production was often erratic and that these figures would not hold good for all years. Bronygarth lime-kilns did not have a siding after 1888.

Mineral Extracted	Quarry: How Loaded	In Operation		Persons employed
		From	To	
Granite quarry	Hendre, gravity	1875	1950	110
Slate mine and quarry	Cambrian, incline	1856	1947	90
Slate mine and quarry	Wynne, incline†	c.1884	1909	70
		1924	1927	15
Granite mine	Coed-y-Glyn, gravity	c.1890	1907	35
Chinastone quarry	Lower Pandy, gravity	c.1885 ⎱		
Chinastone quarry	Caediecws, not direct*	1898 ⎰	1908	15
Granite quarry	Upper Pandy, not direct*	c.1900 ⎰		
Granite quarry	Teirw Hill, gravity	1891	1896	10
Silica quarry	Craig-y-Pandy, gravity	1911	1920	10
Limestone quarry and kilns	Bronygarth, not direct	1770	1920	3

* Feeding to crusher at Lower Pandy Quarry.
† The quarry owned by the Wynne family from early in the 19th century had been producing from about 1750, and much of its output would have gone on to the GVT before it was rail-connected about 1884.

Appendix Four
Officers

Chairmen		Managers	
1873–1886	Lord Arthur Trevor of Brynkinalt (Chirk)	1873–1881	Resident Shropshire Union Canal agent at Chirk
1886–1909	Sir Theodore Martin, K.C.B., K.C.V.O.	1881–1891	Unknown
		1891–1923	Mr George Jenkins
1909–1936	Mr Dyke Dennis (son of Henry Dennis)	1923–1935	Mr Albert Wynn

Sources

Annual returns and reports, 1913–34. GVT Company. File R776, Companies Registration Office, London.

Beyer Peacock & Co. Ltd, Manchester, Locomotive details.

Bradshaw Timetables, 1877–1886, 1900–1933.

Buildings, collection of drawings, scale 1 foot to ⅛ inch. E. Lloyd, 24 Bury St., Hightown, Wrexham.

Byegones, Woodall & Co., Oswestry. These are a set of reprints of notes appearing in newspaper *Oswestry Advertizer*. Occasional references, e.g. July 1881, p. 258.

Byelaws and Regulations. Approved by Board of Trade, June 1897.

Ceiriog Memorial Institute, Glynceiriog. Small collection of relics.

Chirk Track Layout Plan, 1926. Scale 40 feet to 1 inch. Western Region Deeds and Records Office, British Railways, London (now probably in P.R.O., Kew).

Dennis, Henry. *Dictionary of Welsh Biography Down to 1940.* 1959, p. 167.

Ellesmere and Glyn Valley Railways Acts, 1866, 1869, and Evidence.

Glyn Valley Tramway Acts, 1870, 1878, 1885, and Evidence.

History of the Steam Tram, Whitcombe, H.A., Oakwood Press, 1961.

Light Railways, Mackay, C.J. Crosby, Lockwood & Son. 1896. p. 58, 94–99, 240.

Light Railways Investigation Committee. GVT File (C.L.29), 1920. Records Office, Ministry of Transport, London.

Locomotive News and Railway Notes, 10th September, 1919, p. 11. Disposal of ex-LROD Baldwin 60 cm. gauge locomotives.

Martin, Sir Theodore. *Dictionary of National Biography, 2nd Supp. 1901–1911*, p. 575.

Metropolitan-Cammell Carriage & Wagon Co. Ltd, Birmingham. Rolling stock details.

Micro-film Record of Author's Research Data, 1963. Held by National Library of Wales, Aberystwyth.

Ordnance Survey Maps, 25 inches to 1 mile. Denbighshire, Sheets 39 and 40. Original survey, 1872–74 and corrections, 1909–10.

Oswestry and Border Counties Advertizer. Oswestry, Salop. Occasional references, e.g. 18th March, 1891.

Photographs. Minimum of 130 views in existence covering periods: Horse era – 2%, 1888 to 1905 – 14%, 1906 to 1920 – 23%, 1921 to 1935 – 61%.

Printed Memorandum 'Glyn Valley Railway', 3 pp. A form of prospectus explaining profitability of converting line to steam traction. Undated, probably 1885.

Railway Gazette, (a) 21st September, 1920, p. 30–36. 'Light railway working on the Western Front', (b) 27th September, 1934, 6th September and 1st November, 1935, 10th December, 1937; closure details.

Railway Inspectors' report. Index 24565. MT 29/36. Report No. 2716/75, dated 10.4.1875. Public Record Office, Kew.

Railway returns, 1888–1934. B. of T. and M. of T., H.M.S.O. Returns on capital, traffic, receipts, rolling stock, etc.

Shropshire Union Co. Executive Committee Minutes, 1872–1891. British Transport Commission Historical Library, London (now probably in P.R.O., Kew).

Snailbeach District Railways, Tonks, E.S. Published by author. 32 pp. 1950.

Talyllyn Railway Company, Towyn, Merioneth. Two coaches.

Wem and Bronygarth Road Acts, 1856, 1860, 1862, and Evidence.

Wey-Lyn Railway Records (GVT File). Collections of articles, cuttings, early tickets, photographs. BTC Historical Library, London (now in P.R.O., Kew).

Locomotive *Glyn* with closed and open carriages seen here in the goods yard at Glynceiriog about 1900. Note the ornate carriage livery.   *Locomotive Publishing Co.*

Bibliography

References of one full page or more.

ABC Narrow Gauge Railways, Davies, W.J.K., Ian Allan, 1961, p. 43–44.

Beyer Peacock Quarterly Review, Vol. 5, No. 3. July 1931. p. 57–62.

British Narrow Gauge Railways, Jones, R.B., Adam & Charles Black, 1958. p. 40–42.

Ellesmere and Llangollen Canal, E.A. Wilson, Phillimore & Co. Chichester 1975 (pp. 84–90).

The Glyn Valley Tramway, W.J. Milner, Oxford Publishing Co., Poole, 1984.

Glyn Valley Tramway, Parts I, II, III. Milner, W.J. Oswestry Advertizer (newspaper), 21st and 28th August, 4th September, 1957.

Lines of Character, Rolt, L.T.C., and Whitehouse, P.B., Constable, 1952. p. 100–104.

Narrow Gauge Album, Whitehouse, P.B., Ian Allan, 1957. p. 101–103.

Narrow Gauge Rails in Mid Wales, Boyd, J.I.C., Oakwood Press. 146 pp., 1952. Chapter III of 22 pages covers the GVT. This is the most detailed description of the line in this bibliography.

Narrow Gauge Railways of Wales, Kidner, R.W., Oakwood Press, 1947.

Railway Magazine (a) July to December, 1902, p. 322–326. (b) January to June 1912, p. 145–147. (c) January to June, 1926, p. 283–286. (d) November 1934, p. 376. (e) June 1941, p. 280.

Railways, later Railway World March 1943, p. 44–45; April 1951, p. 73; February 1962, p. 68–69.

The Locomotive (Review), Vol. 28, 15th November, 1922. p. 328–329.

Talyllyn News, No. 16, September 1957, p. 1–2; No. 20, September 1958, p. 1–2; No. 29, May 1961, p. 4.

'Twenty years since the Glyn Railway carried its cargo' Saturday Sports News (newspaper), 21st May, 1955.

Acknowledgments

(First Edition)

It was Montaigne who wrote, 'I have gathered a posie of other men's flowers and nothing but the thread that binds them is my own' and these words described exactly my own part in the production of this booklet.

During its lifetime the GVT was little chronicled and during the last war all its official records were pulped. To assemble its history, it has therefore been necessary to consult countless secondary sources and to see those who knew the GVT before its closure. To all those who helped me, as official or private individuals, in important matters or minor detail, go my grateful thanks.

In particular, I wish to acknowledge:

Official Institutions:

Beyer Peacock Gorton Ltd
British Museum Map Room
British Quarrying Co. Ltd
British Transport Commission Historical Library
Ceiriog Memorial Institute
Ceiriog Rural District Council
Companies Registration Office
Deeds and Records Office, Western Region, British Railways

House of Lords Records Office
Metropolitan-Cammell Carriage and Wagon Co. Ltd
Ministry of Transport Library
Narrow Gauge Railway Society
National Library of Wales
Oswestry Public Library
Public Record Office
University of London Periodical Library

Persons living in the locality:

Mr G.R. Beech (Glynceiriog), Mr H.G. Davies (Wrexham), Mrs J. Gander (Bronygarth), Mr C. Hughes (Llangollen), *Mr J.A. Hughes* (Chirk), *Mr D.R. Jones* (Chirk), *Mr J.E. Jones* (Dolywern), Mr C.B. Phillips (Preesgwyn), Mr E.A. Wilson (Ellesmere), and *Mr A. Wynn* (ex-Ruabon). Persons whose names are in italics were one-time employees of the GVT Company.

Railway Researchers:

Messrs C.R. Clinker, S.H.P. Higgins, E. LLoyd, W.J. Milner, D. Newham and A.G. Wells.

Photographs:

Owners who have kindly allowed their illustrations to be included in the text. Individual acknowledgments are given under each photograph.

Plans and Drawings:

Mr Harry Jack deserves a special word of appreciation for all the plans, track diagrams and drawings which are the result of his able draughtsmanship.

London, May 1962.   *David Davies*

(Second Edition)

In preparing the present edition Mike Higgins and The Glyn Valley Tramway Group (founded 1975) have been of great assistance. Details of the Group may be obtained from David Norman, 4 Yew Tree Court, Gresford, Wrexham, Clwyd LL12 8ET. Some additional information has also been supplied by R.W. Kidner.